SPEAK OUT!

Developing Communication and Media Skills

Joanna Crosse

A & C Black

Published 2004
A & C Black Publishers Ltd
37 Soho Square
London W1D 3QZ
www.acblack.com

© Joanna Crosse 2004

ISBN 0 7136 6798 2

A CIP catalogue record for this book is available from the British Library.

A & C Black uses paper produced with elemental chlorine-free pulp, harvested from managed sustainable forests.

Printed and bound in Great Britain by Biddles Ltd, King's Lynn

CONTENTS

To my clients and contributors
without whom this book would not have been possible.

Acknowledgements

I would like to give my heartfelt thanks to my family and friends, who supported and encouraged me to 'Speak Out'. Firstly a hug to my three children, Skye, Merrick, and Sedona, who heard the cry 'I must write my book' for the best part of a year!

Thanks to my mother Jennifer Shennan and dear friend Caroline Mercier for being there for me. To Jim Ferguson for his contribution in the media skills section of the book and to my lovely editor Jessica Hodge, who inspired me to find my voice through this project.

1. VOICE
How to Use Your Voice to the Full

The voice is a wonderful instrument and, like any musical instrument, we can play it well or badly. Our voice is an expression of who we are. The more effectively we use our voice, the more powerful our message. It is an expression of identity, personality, even self-esteem. What does a flat, dull voice suggest to you? Or what about the person who whispers and doesn't really own their voice? Equally, a strident or harsh voice can make a person seem aggressive or opinionated.

We can spend time and money on ourselves so we look good but how often do we consider the impact we make when we open our mouths? After training with people in both the media and corporate sector, it is apparent to me that there are fundamental truths about how we use our voice, whatever walk of life we come from.

Fiona is a continuity announcer and voiceover artist and she made a pertinent observation about the human voice during a coaching session.

'People often take great care about their appearance. They buy the right clothes, go to the hairdresser, have a manicure, slim and tone up. But the one thing we all take for granted is our voice! Yet it's such an important part of our image. Imagine a beautiful woman entering a room and all eyes turning on her, but as soon as she opens her mouth the illusion is shattered!

For an announcer who is heard and not seen, it is all the more important to develop a warm, friendly voice which is easy to listen to. We have to encourage our audience to listen without the hard sell. Voice lessons can help you to use your voice to its full capacity and coaching will help you to become aware of your voice. It is not just professionals who benefit from a clear, concise delivery. Finding your voice can increase your confidence and self-image and helps people in all walks of life.'

I think Fiona makes a crucial point. Finding your voice is absolutely essential whatever your situation. I have discovered over the years that helping people work with their voices often starts at home. Finding the right words to say in a family or social situation can be just as challenging as presenting a speech at a conference.

Our voice is such an intimate part of ourselves that it is often difficult to find the right words and the right way of saying something to represent who we really are. How many times have you felt unheard or misunderstood? It's not just what you say, it's the way you say it.

I remember having problems with a large telecommunications company over several months. Every time I rang to complain, I voiced my complaints in a reasonable and compliant way. Each time I was greeted by a friendly customer service representative who told me in the most reassuring tone of voice that it would all be sorted out. But as the months went by still nothing was resolved and I still had problems with my telephone. I called again for the umpteenth time and the voice on the other end of the phone was polite but cold. The woman assured me everything was being done but because of her dismissive, patronising tone of voice I didn't believe her and I felt she didn't care. I put the phone down feeling angry and that pushed me into making a serious complaint. Guess what? The problem was resolved within days.

When I reflected on what had happened I realised it was not what the customer service woman had said but the way in which she'd said it that had moved me to take action. I believe that how we speak is the foundation stone of a clear and direct message.

In this chapter, we will explore using our voices in terms of pitch, pace and sound, but on a more fundamental level we need to understand how our voice can be a real barometer of the way we feel about ourselves.

In the work I do I have come across people who potentially have wonderful voices but are frightened of using them properly. It's almost as if they're in awe of speaking their own truth.

One such person is Les. An attractive, seemingly confident and self-possessed woman.

'You would have thought at the age of 36 I could find somewhere to to cry other than my living room floor – but no – I found myself gravitating towards the 'black stuff' in a very undignified and crumpled heap. Oh, how I wish I'd hoovered!

The cause of these tears? Being dumped by my knight in shining Armani? That ever-elusive size 6? No. These tears were caused by somebody showing an interest and taking time and talking to me. How, in a two-minute conversation, does that somebody work you out when for all these years you've tried so incredibly hard to keep the real you hidden?

Joanna noticed something in me even I didn't know I had – or did I? Some people lose their purse, their diary or car keys. Joanna realised very early on in my somewhat breathy conversation that I had lost something far more accessible – my voice. Not chosen to read aloud at school because my voice sounded 'too low', I had remained hidden silently at the back of the class. And for the past 36 years that is where my sound had stayed.

During our first 'black session' Joanna let me cry. During the second session Joanna talked and during the third we talked. Over time I was encouraged to speak, not just with words but with confidence. Where had this 'new' voice come from? More importantly had it always been there?

For me my journey has been about two things. Discovering myself and finding the right path with my voice at the end of it. I haven't got there yet, wherever 'there' may be. But even I can recognise the progress that's been made. I haven't been 'somewhere over the rainbow' and I still haven't found what I'm looking for but with the right help, encouragement and self-belief, I have found the confidence to speak and ask for directions.'

Owning our voice is about owning who we are.

VOICE PREPARATION: BREATHING AND RELAXATION

But first things first. How can we possibly make the best use of our voice if we don't know how to breathe properly? Have you ever noticed that when you're frightened or tensed up your breathing changes? In fact, when we're really under pressure what sometimes happens is that we stop breathing altogether – we put our breath on hold!

I think it's symbolic that we do that. Breathing is about living. Breathing is about owning our right to be in the world. Using our voice powerfully is about our right to have our say. Breathing is both life-giving, and fundamental to how we speak and use our voice.

Because it's something we take for granted we probably don't take much notice of how we breathe. One thing is for certain: we take air into our lungs morning, noon and night without even thinking about it. It's our life force. But how we breathe is also important. Shallow breathing can be a symbol of our fear of life, our fear of really living our life. Taking deep breaths and feeling centred and rooted to the earth is about being here and living our life. So first things first: learn to breathe properly.

To be able to breathe in a relaxed way is something you may have to work at. We all live our lives in such a hectic frantic way it's like being on fast forward. Learning to breathe properly and slow down is about pressing the pause button and then moving into play mode.

What might be relaxing for one person won't necessarily be so for another. Even giving yourself time to go for a swim or a walk or to take some other form of exercise can help you to slow down and give you time to think and take stock of things. That very act in itself is relaxing.

Exercise
Try sitting in a chair and just being. Watch all those busy thoughts float past. Observe them rather than being involved with them. This is a good way of being able to disconnect from the negative thought patterns that we all carry. Learn to be the observer and that in turn will help you feel more in control of what's going on.

Meditation, yoga, or some form of martial arts which helps connect mind, body and spirit, are all excellent ways of taking time out and bringing us into balance. Being able to get back into balance is important in terms of using our voice. If it is an expression of who we are, then we have to learn to be still and centred to be able to produce the best possible sounds our voice can make.

Exercise

Try lying on the floor with your head on a cushion or pillow and close your eyes. For a start I bet this isn't a luxury you allow yourself very often, if at all, so taking time out, even for just ten minutes, can be a real boost and help you through the day.

Start by taking in a nice deep breath and at the same time feel your ribcage expand. Breathe in deeply and hold for a second before breathing out. Imagine you are breathing in pure, fresh, life-giving air and breathing out any old unwanted stale air. The more deeply you can breathe in and hold for a second or two and then breathe out, the more relaxed you will start to feel.

Breathing connects us to the moment. If we are in the moment, we are not worrying about something we did yesterday or being scared of what tomorrow brings. Breathing brings us back to the here and now and helps us feel connected.

In terms of using our voice, the more breath we have the easier it makes our delivery. Breathing properly helps us to stay in control of what we're saying and it means we're going slowly enough to put real expression into our voice. When we're nervous or tense our breathing becomes rapid and we find ourselves breathing from our chest, or even through our nose, and that in turn makes our voices sound higher, squeakier and less meaningful.

Sounding calm, confident and conversational starts with good breathing.

Exercise

Try this exercise either standing, or sitting with both feet on the ground. Close your eyes and imagine your breath coming from the very centre of your being. Inhale deeply and gradually let the breath out as far as it will go. Feel all that tension and stress move out of your body. Do this for a minute or two and you will notice you feel calmer, more relaxed and centred.

Now as you keep breathing nice and deeply imagine your feet are rooted to the ground. In fact I want you to feel the roots going into the ground. It will give you an immediate feeling of being connected to the earth: grounded. If we're grounded and in the moment, then we are absolutely in control of ourselves and what we're going to say.

It's worth being aware of your stomach because this is the very centre of your being. This is also known as the solar plexus area, a complex network of nerves at the pit of the stomach, Hence the expression 'butterflies in the stomach'; it's where our body responds physically to emotions generated by events going on around us. This in turn of course can have other physical repercussions, and there's more about this in the section on Physical Problems later in this chapter.

Feeling nervous doesn't just make us feel sick or anxious in our stomach but it has a knock-on effect with our voice. It basically means we start to breathe from the upper part of our body rather than taking deep breaths from the centre of our being. Learning to breathe more deeply and from the stomach helps calm our nerves, keeps us connected and in turn brings our voice down into the centre of our being and enables us to create a more vibrant, colourful sound.

Think of your voice as a palette of twenty-five colours. Most of us probably only use about five colours out of the possible twenty-five. The voice has extraordinary range, depth and colour. It's the difference between a pastel picture and a canvas of bright and vivid colours. Each will have a different impact on how we feel about ourselves and how the person or people hearing us will respond.

WHAT DOES YOUR VOICE SAY ABOUT YOU?

Research has shown that, in terms of how our speech is received by our hearers, 38 per cent of our success is down to how we sound. What we say accounts for only 7 per cent. Body language of course plays a major role, coming in at 55 per cent. But having said that, if you're on the end of a telephone it doesn't count for anything. So how we sound is vital to how our message is being heard. In other words we need to match our message.

I still work as a broadcast journalist and train other reporters and presenters on a regular basis so I am only too well aware of the importance of delivery. Some journalists have a problem with putting emotion into their scripts. They are concerned that they will sound biased or prejudiced in some way. I always point out that they're either reading a sad story, a tale with a businesslike message or a light-hearted story. The words need somehow to be pumped up with the right emotion. You can't have a tragedy that sounds like a comedy. Equally, it's inappropriate to drone your way through something that's meant to amuse or delight.

Putting it simply, when we have natural, spontaneous conversations with people we don't usually think about how we're speaking – we're just speaking. We are naturally expressive. There's lots of highs and lows and different colours put onto our picture because we are telling a story. We are involved in the story-telling and in some ways become part of it.

I bet you can always tell when someone isn't listening to you. Equally, it's pretty easy to guess when somebody isn't really thinking about what they're saying. It's like they are somehow disconnected. Imagine you are on the phone to someone and having an animated conversation. Then the person on the other line quietly puts the phone down and wanders off. You might not know that for sure but you can feel there is no-one there. They have disconnected. In the same way, if you disconnect from your message the listener will sense that. And then they in turn will lose interest.

It's all about sounding real. And you can only sound real if you are there in the moment.

Imagine your voice is carried on a sound wave, which of course it is. That wave somehow has a magnetic quality that will attract someone to it. If that energy connection is broken, the sound won't reach the recipient. That is what I believe happens when people lose their connection with their message and it translates in the way their voice sounds.

For many people their voice is their hang-up. Not surprising, really, when you consider the voice is such an intimate part of ourselves. Our voice can say so much, or so little. I think subconsciously many people are aware of this and it holds them back from speaking out.

I have yet to meet someone who hasn't disliked hearing their own voice back – even cringed - at least for the first few times. Let me reassure you that this is completely normal! But the sense of excruciating embarrassment does pass and after you have heard your voice played back a few times you can hear yourself without feeling self-conscious.

It's almost as if your outer ear has a different experience from your inner ear. You know when you feel it just doesn't sound like you? Well, that's because you've always been used to listening to your voice on the inside rather than the outside. But once you've got used to hearing your voice as others hear it then you can live much more easily with the sound of your own voice.

For anybody who feels they have some kind of speech impediment, using their voice to its full potential can be a real challenge. But it is possible. I have met and worked with people who have overcome the most extraordinary vocal challenges and ended up as broadcasters or working in an area where they constantly have to talk to lots of other people.

Bob is a professional television presenter with thirty years experience in the industry. But in his childhood he developed a bad stutter.

'I have no idea which caused it….the stutter just started one day. My childhood was pretty idyllic, brought up in Cape Town with the run of a mountainside every day. My first memory of the speech problem is a year or two before my parents fled the nationalist/apartheid regime and came back to Britain. I must have been about nine. School was the Christian Brothers' College in Cape Town, run by a bunch of sadistic priests who took great pleasure in shoving gutteral Afrikaans down our throats and making us rugby tackle on the concrete playground. There wasn't much of God's loving from them. They took delight, great delight, in mocking my stutter and making me embarrassed in front of my classmates. I wasn't exactly sad to leave the South African education system and enter a good old British grammar school.

By then of course the stutter was bad. And I mean bad. Speaking in class was a huge effort. I had the answers to questions in my head but could never get them out. I spiralled down, I suppose putting things down on paper rather than tackling them verbally. The first part of my secondary education consisted of dark days, gagged by my inability to communicate. For a blonde youngster speaking with a South African accent and just beginning to feel testosterone, it was more than frustrating, it was almost fatal.

One of two things began to appear as lifesavers. My accent, when I was relaxed and could get the words out, was attractive to classmates, and girls! So I played on that. In fact I increased the accent and that helped with the stutter.

Another way of coping was to let my body do the talking. Not some perverse sexual athlete at the age of spotty thirteen but as a rugby player. It's the only thing I can thank the primeval priests for. They taught me to be as hard as nails with their concrete rugby pitch. I could rugby tackle an elephant and it wouldn't get up afterwards. I could charge through the opposition like going through a herd of wildebeest. In my eyes the opposing team were lemmings to be disposed of. I could drop a schoolboy rugby player at fifty yards just by looking at him, after that first tackle where I imposed my physical presence in no uncertain terms. To get up from the pitch by pushing on his head and uttering the Afrikaaner-style words, 'Argh, man next time I will break bones', had an amazing effect not only on the quivering opponents but also on my popularity generally. I wasn't that hot on talking but then who cares if you have 'jockstrap appeal'.

This idea of hiding behind a physical disguise I suppose grew in my mind and I think this encouraged me to take the boldest step yet. I joined the school drama club.

This would really make me speak in public. It was only possible because I was playing a role, it wasn't really me. Step out of the role and I was a gibbering, stammering wreck; behind the greasepaint I could be someone else. That person could be confident, outspoken, verbose. It was brilliant. I couldn't wait to learn more parts; rehearsals were sweet; performances were just orgasmic! Brutus in Shakespeare, Charles Condomine in Noel Coward – hopefully I was word perfect. The prompter was out of business with me!

After school it was straight into a business that forced me to converse with people – journalism. To say I was scared is the understatement of the century. I couldn't hide behind anything. I had to be myself and confront the stutter, mouth to mouth. I worked on a little weekly newspaper doing my three-year apprenticeship,. Bottom of the food chain, but I was forced to face my impediment and try to overcome it. There'd been no help from anyone else. Not once was I referred to a psychiatrist, analyst or specialist. I was left to do it on my own.

Silly things like conversations on the telephone were enormous problems for me. I struggled to get the words out – not good for a rookie reporter trying to make his name. And just saying my name could be a block. I was in nervous meltdown.

But once having got the facts, I had a knack of being able to put them in the right order on paper. I think the writing skills pulled me through. Slowly confidence came and with it the rewards – qualifications. Time to move on.

The ultimate challenge was to get into television journalism. My father was a TV anchorman for a regional BBC station. I aspired to that but certainly didn't want any help from him to achieve it. Again the only way to conquer the nerves and the resulting stammer was to think of my reporting work as a role, similar to acting. I used to put on this hard news voice to convince myself that it was someone else, not me. It worked, and continued to work when I presented.

In the old days at this regional television station we used to do live voiceovers on news items. That was a real test. Sometimes I had a waver on air – a stammer or a fluff. It would stay with me for days. It would torture me – I would be fearful that the carefully nurtured confidence would evaporate away. But I found the increasing number of days when I put good pieces together or did 'lives' without the slightest quiver in the voice were intoxicating.

To keep overcoming this mystery handicap is now a daily addiction. It's the challenge of maintaining confidence. Things can affect it – stress in my personal or home life can undermine it. Then I have to slip into the role-playing again to climb back up that slope. I would say without doubt that facing it and confronting it with the severest test of all has helped me to move on successfully from my stuttering start in life.'

Shyness is something that affects many people and it can be debilitating or in some cases it can provide a launch pad for life.

Isabel is a seventy two year old retired Scottish school teacher.

'I have lived with problems of shyness all my life, but I have refused to allow them to be a barrier to accomplishing my aims in life. I was the quiet pupil who would never draw attention to myself and hated being asked to read aloud or take part in any performances.

Before my schooldays were over I knew that I must take steps to control my shyness and limit its effect on my life. My parents discussed the career choices suitable for their shy, bookworm daughter and thought that office work or becoming a librarian might suit my temperament. But I rejected these options because I felt they pandered to my weakness. I told them that if I became a librarian I had a vision of myself disappearing down the aisles of the National Library never to surface in human company again. I had to take a job which would bring me into contact with people. So I decided to become a teacher.

I discovered I was not a natural born teacher. I had to be a made one, but not entirely self-made. My college tutors were able to give me advice and training in voice projection, body language, the meticulous preparation of lessons and techniques of engaging with pupils. None of this was easy for me and fifty years on I have not forgotten the painful lessons when I had to teach pupils under the watchful eye of tutor, headmaster or inspector. Almost as bad was enduring the criticisms themselves. But it worked. I learned to stand in front of an indifferent audience and make an acceptable presentation.

I also joined an amateur dramatic society, which I enjoyed and it helped me with voice production and confidence. On stage you are somebody else and not exposing your own personality to the audience.

Being shy isn't always a disadvantage. The shy person is more inclined to stand back and observe others which can help in developing a deeper understanding of human motives and behaviour. The shy person guards against being taken by surprise or at a disadvantage. If you habitually arrive on time and meet your deadlines, you do not need to blush and stammer and produce lame excuses. If you meticulously prepare and know your facts, you can withstand pressure and avoid the traps that catch those who rely on inspiration to cover the gaps in their information. I found that the very techniques I used to cope with my shyness led to my gaining a successful career and a good reputation as a teacher.'

We can speak up for ourselves and give voice to our opinions. We can also choose how we use our voice. Will it emanate harmonious notes or sound flat, dull and uninteresting?

Imagine, whatever your situation, you are telling one person a story. In essence that is the truth of the matter. Whether you are giving a presentation to hundreds, chairing a business meeting or having a conversation with one individual, it is important to make sure every person on the receiving end of your words feels as if you are talking to them alone. Get them hooked in so they are hanging on your every word!

YOUR VOICE IS HOW YOU FEEL

In my experience as a broadcast journalist and presenter coupled with training media professionals for many years, the essential basis for being able to use your voice confidently and effectively is self-esteem. How we feel about ourselves has a huge impact on how we are heard and how we sound.

How do you see yourself: if you looked in the mirror who would reflect back at you? Would it be a confident optimistic person who believes in themselves, or someone who feels they're not quite good enough? How we see ourselves is very often not the way others see us.

There is that great saying 'fake it to make it'. To a certain degree that works because the more we act 'as if', the more likely we are to be what we're trying to be. But wouldn't it be great if our feelings on the inside were the same as the feelings on the outside?

Having worked both with top business people in the corporate world and experienced television presenters, I can vouch for the fact that all of us at some time or another, whatever our position in life, have wondered if we're going to be 'found out'. It is quite normal to question ourselves. This only becomes damaging to our self-esteem when we really cannot see our qualities and abilities. I believe that feeling OK about who we are and our place in the world is critical to our self-esteem and therefore to using our voice.

It's down to personal responsibility. Looking after ourselves on a physical, emotional, mental and even spiritual level can and does have a profound effect on how we live our lives.

How do you feel if someone pays you a compliment? Do you accept it with grace or dismiss it? Many years ago, someone told me that to dismiss a compliment is to insult the person who is trying to pay it and that it is arrogant to suggest you know better than them. For example if someone says: 'You look great today,' you might reply, 'Thanks very much, I'm feeling good.'

But someone with low self-esteem might say: 'Oh no I don't, I'm having a bad hair day and look dreadful!' I daresay the person who paid the compliment wouldn't be in a big hurry to pay another one.

Assertiveness

Learning to be assertive and to get our needs met in life is fundamental to how we are seen in the world. Whilst the person who says yes to everyone and takes on the world's problems is probably a popular and likeable member of staff, you can bet a lot of the time they're not feeling that good about themselves. It's important to have boundaries for yourself and know when to say yes and when to say no. Not only that: it's vital to learn how to say yes and no effectively enough to be heard.

I truly believe that the world would be a different place – and a better one – if all of us could take responsibility for ourselves. We seem to live in a blame culture where it's easier to find fault in others rather than look at ourselves. Taking personal responsibility starts at the basic level of what we feel on the inside and the kind of language we use.

Being assertive is about being honest and having clear, direct communication. It's not about blaming others or being controlling or bossy. It's a much more genial way of communicating. For example, not demanding of others but asking. Not demeaning or dumping but offering constructive criticism. Simply, being assertive is about respecting oneself and others.

It's not just how we say something, of course, but the way in which we say it. One of the most powerful ways of speaking our truth and commanding respect from others is owning what we say. How many times have you heard people talk about 'you' or 'we' when they're expressing something they feel; something which is their opinion rather than yours. Personally, I find it difficult when I hear someone telling me, through their inappropriate language, how I feel when really they're talking about themselves.

It's such a powerful feeling to own what you say. Using the 'I' word rather than the 'you' or ' we' words. It also means that the person on the receiving end can really hear what you're saying because it belongs to you. If they feel dragged into your opinions, especially when they conflict with their own, it can lead to them feeling angry or put out and then they're not in a position to hear what you've got to say.

Here are some techniques to try out:
- Remember you only have to take responsibility for what you have to say and not for someone else.
- It's about mutual respect, not about winning or beating them.
- You are not looking for their approval.
- You just have to be yourself, honest and direct.
- Language: use 'I' – I think. I feel. In my experience.
- Be clear.
- Be direct.
- Learn to take a breath and pause.
- Know what your message is.
- Hear what the other person has to say.
- Be willing to compromise but know your boundaries.

Owning your statements helps you to be aware of your feelings and to respond in a clearer and more authentic way. Remember, nobody can judge or blame you for having feelings, because they're your feelings and nobody else's. You have rights just like anyone else. You have the right to your feelings and the right to express your beliefs and opinions. You have the right to ask for what you need and also the right to change your mind.

In a conflict situation there's a useful technique that can help you to be clear and direct and in turn helps the other person to hear what you're saying without feeling blamed.

For example:
- When you did that ... I felt
- That experience left me feeling
- I felt ... when this happened ...

Aggressive behaviour

I am sure that at some time or another you have been on the receiving end of aggressive behaviour. When someone lashes out at you or blames you for something you haven't done. Often it's the way in which it's said that can be the most damaging. Aggressive behaviour can make you feel blamed, put down or even threatened. Aggressive behaviour is when someone gets into your body space, when you feel invaded verbally or physically. You feel as though they're in some competition. They need to win at all costs and your feelings and opinions aren't even considered.

It's probably not necessary to give examples because unfortunately many people resort to aggressive behaviour when they feel insecure and don't know how to communicate properly. It's when someone expresses their opinion as fact and that in its very essence makes you 'wrong'; it's when they sound harsh, angry, sarcastic, use invasive, aggressive body language and don't leave any space verbally or physically for you to reply.

It's worth remembering that most people resort to aggressive behaviour when they feel frightened, defensive or insecure. If we're clear and confident about what we've got to say then there's no need to be pushy or demanding. If we're confident about what we feel on the inside it doesn't necessarily matter what the person who's on the receiving end thinks or feels.

Which takes us nicely on to the subject of passive behaviour.

Passive behaviour

It's a myth that never saying no and always saying yes to please others is altogether a good thing. It may make us popular and likeable but how do we end up feeling about ourselves? How many times have you said yes when you really meant no? How many times have you felt you haven't been heard? That can make us feel undervalued and simply not good enough.

In fact passive behaviour really means we're playing the victim role. People often use the expression 'being a doormat.' You know the person who can't stand up for themselves, the one that's exploited and put upon by other people.

I once heard the expression 'exploding doormat' which I thought was a brilliant description for someone playing the passive role. Feeling angry but not being able to acknowledge or express it can lead to simmering feelings of resentment, anger, self-pity and victimisation, which fester away and invariably leak out.

Ever been around someone who appears to be very sweet and willing but actually you pick up some sense of their resentment? Unexpressed feelings and an inability to set boundaries can create very negative feelings which, if undealt with, become toxic and block us from communicating clearly with others.

I honestly used to think going along with the majority, keeping everybody happy, was at least better that being aggressive or inappropriately angry. Today, I'm not so sure. Having still to deal with my own tendency towards passive behaviour, I know how unhealthy it is to hang onto negative feelings or not to express myself directly.

Can you remember a time when you've walked away from a confrontational or hostile situation fantasising in your head what you would really have liked to say rather than what you did or didn't say? You can pretty much bet you were being passive.

So to sum up passive behaviour, it's when you lack self-esteem and may behave in a victimised way; being helpless or complaining that somehow all the odds are stacked against you. In other words it's when you feel powerless and display powerlessness. It's when you are over-apologetic and over-placatory. Saying sorry and thanks is great but not in excess. Over-using them somehow undermines what they mean and can make you look insincere.

I was born an apologiser! As a result I've had to spend many years trying not to say the 'S' word. My children are always great teachers. If I ever force them to say sorry for some misdemeanour they simply turn round and say 'why should we say sorry, if we don't mean it'. I think that's absolutely right, even saying good words insincerely means we are not being honest or truthful.

Often how we speak and the words we use can be a barometer of how we're feeling on the inside. Although I rarely over-apologise these days – on the basis that I have to walk my talk! - when I do lapse into old behaviour patterns and start my 'sorry syndrome' or put myself down, I know it's time to take a look at what's going on inside.

Indirect behaviour

This is when you avoid communicating clearly and you beat about the bush so the person on the receiving end doesn't really know what you're getting at. Again, it's all about the need to avoid confrontation and in a sense to avoid speaking your truth. Ethical behaviour surely is partly about being who we are, owning who we are. Not speaking your truth, however painful, is a lie. I was shocked when I realised that avoiding talking my truth was in essence unethical behaviour. And yet we can often resort to manipulation to avoid having to speak the truth.

But if you don't take the risk of communicating clearly then, just as with passive behaviour, you will hold onto unhealthy feelings and end up lashing out at the person or situation eventually anyway. I remember years ago an American therapist gave me some very sound advice which I have used ever since.

Imagine that you have a little book. Every time you don't deal with a problem or grievance, a stamp of resentment goes into your book. You haven't said anything to anybody, and nobody as far as you are concerned knows you have any worries whatsoever.

We carry on putting our stamps of resentment into our little book, avoiding dealing with painful issues and confronting our concerns. The only problem is the book of stamps is getting fuller. One day somebody asks us to do something – like any other day of the week – and as far as we're concerned they've gone one step too far. Guess what? The last stamp has gone into the book and we explode!

All around us look horrified and wonder what on earth is going on. We're behaving out of character, expressing months, years even, of accumulated resentments all in one go. Like some festering volcano that has just exploded at ten on the Richter scale! And nobody likes it. They haven't seen us like that before and they really don't want to see us like this now. Apart from anything else it looks like we're being totally unreasonable about some trivial issue.

Only trouble is, it isn't just one small thing we've exploded about. It's all the other stamps in the book. I often remember this and, if confronted with a difficult situation, I try to remind myself that not dealing effectively with something is only storing up trouble for later on.

Indirect behaviour is in essence avoiding confronting something head on or directly. So try to avoid skirting the issue, dropping hints or just plain hoping the other person knows how you're feeling. Only you can take responsibility for getting your needs met and saying what you need to say.

Maurice is a professional in his twenties. A charming guy, popular at work, with lots of friends. His one real handicap is his inability to say no.

'I'm like anyone else; I like to be liked. I like to feel needed, to feel useful and most of all I guess to feel valued. It's what gets me through. It's my crutch and ironically the one character flaw which drops me on my ass more than anything else. Needing to be liked, to feel worthy, leaves me feeling like I can't say no. Now, I'm not weak, I'm just conscious of the fact that everyone has needs. I have just never believed mine are as important as those around me.

I can find a lot of excuses for being me – the way I am. Is it being raised as a guilt-ridden Catholic that's left me desperate to justify my existence? Being the youngest of a big and poor Irish family? Or being the only surviving son in a brood of over-achieving sisters? Who knows, but the result is I feel like I've got to earn my right to be here, my right to be happy.

Like a lot of people I often feel the successes I've enjoyed – am enjoying – are far greater than my actual talent or intellect. I'm not so much deserving as just plain lucky. It may sound ungrateful but it's not always a blessing to be lucky. It comes with its problems. I fear that luck is going to run out. Someone, or worse everyone, is soon going to notice that I'm neither wise nor gifted – I'm just charmed.

To cover my tracks or to keep off everyone's radar, I work hard. Not just at work but in all aspects of my life. I'm compulsive in my inability to relax, to find time for me. While the people I work with seem to succeed for doing just 'their job', I feel I've got to do more. Being average isn't good enough – it doesn't show that I'm justifying the air I waste, the space I take up or the good fortune I've enjoyed.

So if there's extra hours to be worked, I'll work them. If there's another project to do, I'll do it and usually without taking time off rota. I'll take it alongside my existing work. I'll tackle it in my lunch hour or at the weekend. I'll think of it in the shower, driving to work or while cooking dinner. The extra things I take on aren't small. Recently they've ranged from representing the city I live near in its battle to become the European Capital of Culture, to designing and actually rebuilding a community garden – all whilst renovating my own house, working more than full-time hours, studying part-time and trying to be a caring boyfriend, a good son, a true friend and a star employee.

I'm not an egotist (and yeah, I know that's what all egotists say, but really I'm not). I don't take on more to be recognised for it. I don't enjoy being singled out for praise. In fact it makes me feel worse – like it says to the whole room that the only reason I took on more, went further or worked harder was to get public praise. To me that's just shallow.

Any of my friends will tell you I've got an agile mind and a quick wit that could slice ice from two hundred paces. But while I work hard to show the world my charming and happy side, underneath I'm full of resentment. I hate hating myself and I hate the lengths I make myself go to feel better about being me.

The problem is that my problems become other people's problems. Whilst I'm working so hard to please everyone, I actually end up winding myself up. Those closest to me have to endure my endless worry that I'm going to fail and, far worse, perfect strangers sometimes innocently suffer the fallout. I'm not being dramatic, it's true. While it's my boss, my colleagues or my family who take advantage of my compulsion to please, it's the call-centre workers, the despondent check-out girl or the driver in front I take it out on.

Most recently it was the Jehovah's Witness. I had just arrived home from work – two hours later than I should have. I should have had time to eat, shower, change and drive ten miles to meet a crisis-stricken friend, but because I'd stayed on at work I now had only ten minutes. Rather than let my friend down and ring to say I'd be late. I thought 'hey I'll make it. I always do.'

Just as I'd turned the shower on, the doorbell rang. Before me stood an unlikely couple. A tank-topped man with gelled hair and a woman wearing a straw hat and gingham dress. In their hand was a book – I didn't need to see its title. Before either of them said a word I asked if they were Jehovah's Witnesses. They sweetly said yes.

And for their honesty I unleashed on them my very own fury. I told them, as someone who had deliberately turned my back on God (an extremely lapsed Catholic after all) that I didn't appreciate being bugged on my own doorstep by social misfits. I asked them if my house had deliberately been put on some 'God-bothering trail' because they were the fourth pair of Witnesses I'd escorted off my drive in the last year. I sent them back to their Kingdom Hall with a warning that if they or any more of their kind ever darkened my door to peddle their cult again, I'd make them so sorry they'd see Hell as respite.

Why so evil? Not because I'm a Satan worshipper, simply because they were the last stamp in my book.

I was late, hungry, tired and irritable. I had too much on my plate and answering the door to them was not only inconvenient; in my mind it was the single act that day which was going to make me late for my needy friend. Of course I was over-reacting and misdirecting my anger. It was because my work colleagues hadn't pulled their weight that I had to stay on to cover at work. It was because some xxxx in a Mercedes had cut me up so that I got stuck behind a red light and it was because of my lacking the strength to say no at work that I was late at all. But no, in my head these caring, gentle folk were the problem and I wanted them to know it.

My friends laugh when I tell them this tale but I feel shame. My failing to say no is self-destructive. I boil over because I'm working too hard to please everyone and to be liked. But once I've boiled over I hate myself more and feel bad for what I've done. So I take on more to make amends to make up for behaving so badly – starting the cycle all over again.

My real problems are all based in perception. I know how I view myself. I know there's the way people *actually* view me and then there's my Problem – how I *think* people view me. I feel that if I say no, I'll be criticised for lacking drive, for lacking enthusiasm, for being lazy or complacent.

But you know what? Today's Friday. My boss just asked me to work the late shift tonight because someone called in sick. I said no. I didn't say why I couldn't do it. I just said I couldn't. Did she hit the roof? No. Did she hit me? No. Curse at me? Hex me behind my back? Rue the day she ever employed me? No, no and no. She said okay and asked someone else.

I got my evening to myself and had a Jehovah's Witness turned up I'd have had time to tell him politely and simply that whilst I respected him for having a faith, his wasn't for me. And I would wish him well.'

TAKING CONTROL

Without getting into quantum physics, I like the idea of the world being made up of waves of energy. Just as we switch a radio on and listen to a particular station on a particular wavelength, in a sense it's the same with our thoughts and feelings. When we are feeling strong and positive on the inside then somehow that manifests on the outside. Of course we have to learn to speak clearly and directly but our message is 100 per cent clear if we believe or feel what we're saying. Think positively and you will act positively. Think negatively and you will get negative consequences.

Kate Bird is a teacher of assertiveness skills but came to this work, like many of us, through her own personal and sometimes bitter experience.

'Assertiveness. It's such an awful word, isn't it? Images immediately spring to mind of over-confident, overbearing, forceful people who know how to say all the right things so they get exactly what they want, when they want it. Sometimes it looks like manipulation, sometimes it looks like aggression, sometimes it's just plain bossiness. And generally, it's not a behaviour pattern most people want to emulate.

Another view of assertiveness is that it's just a bunch of techniques. The sort of thing you go on management training courses for and get excited about because it makes such sense. Then you get back to work and quickly forget all about it. Firstly, you're too busy and you simply don't have time to recall the step-by-step instructions. And secondly, although the changes you need to make in your communication style appear to be easy, you've discovered assertiveness doesn't work too well when you use it simply as a set of off-the-shelf techniques for managing other people.

This is because it is not a superficial veneer. In its essence, assertiveness is a meaningful set of core-life skills which give you direct access to your own emotional intelligence and help you to say what you mean – and mean what you say – from a place of strength, compassion, integrity, congruity and straightforwardness. As a result your self-esteem increases, you feel much better about yourself and, consequently, more able to act and speak as the strong, mature, gracious and well-balanced person you know you truly are (yes you are!).

And, like most things that are worth having, it takes quite a bit of reflection and practice to truly understand the beauty, value and holism of assertiveness, and to let it become part of your cellular being rather than only an uncomfortable piece of armour to don when you find yourself in an awkward situation.

Nevertheless, there are awkward and difficult situations to be faced tomorrow and you are probably fed up with your own inability to handle them well, usually beating yourself up afterwards. For what? Saying the same old thing that triggers the other person? Going over the top again? Or avoiding the issue again? Or letting yourself be trodden on – again? You know there has got to be a different way to do it or say it, but you can't figure it out for yourself. That's why most people turn up at one of my assertiveness classes – because they are sick of going round in circles with certain individuals, either at home or at work, and are *desperate* (the word most people use) to find a way out of their distress and difficulty.

Which is exactly how I discovered assertiveness. At the age of 44 I found myself working with another woman, a few years younger, whose aggressive retorts and combative manner constantly left me feeling utterly defeated, speechless, put down, and, worst of all, stupid and useless. Even so, I was more furious with myself than her because, in every encounter, I saw I was letting myself down and behaving like a real wimp! I knew I didn't want to pick up my own verbal weapons and go into battle with this woman, but I did want to stand up for myself and speak out in more healthy and self-respecting ways. And, most importantly, to do it without compromising my own quiet and peace-loving self.

Eventually, on one day I clearly remember about eight years ago, my unvoiced desperation with my own doormat behaviour made me get into the car, drive directly to the nearest bookshop and find a book, any book, on assertiveness skills. There was only one on the shelf, so I bought it, went home – and couldn't put it down. *A Woman in Your Own Right*, by Anne Dickson, is one of those books that looks mildly interesting on the outside, but is electrifying to read. It certainly changed my life. Shortly after reading it I trained for a year as an assertiveness teacher, specifically qualified to deliver all the material in Anne's book (which, although first published 21 years ago, is still regarded around the world as the core textbook on assertiveness).

So what are the most useful assertiveness skills? Everyone has a different set of difficult situations to deal with. One woman may find complaining about faulty goods is no problem at all, but the same woman crumples when she's faced with saying no to friends or family. Another may fly off the handle when criticised at work – even when it's fair criticism – and then agonise over how to give legitimate feedback to someone else. Another may be a tough supervisor at work - but gives in on everything to her children at home.

A good place to start is to make a list of your ten most difficult situations, and then put them in order of difficulty. Look on this list as your personal programme. It can be from any area of your life and cover all your relationships, whether personal, social or job-related – in shops or at home, at work or with your neighbours, with your parents, partner or children. Just looking at that list will probably be an eye-opener. Next, write down how you currently behave in each of those circumstances – are you aggressive, passive or manipulative? There is no judgement implied here, we have all got a set of learned behaviours which once protected us very well and were necessary for our survival. But if they no longer serve us and are actually causing us difficulty instead, then it is time to change them. Recognising them, facing them and naming them is, I believe, 95 per cent of bringing about this change. The other five per cent is practising a healthy new way of doing it until it becomes your easy and natural response to the difficulty.

Now number the ten situations in order of difficulty, with your No.10 as the easiest to tackle, and your No. 1 as the most difficult, the one that has you shuddering with horror at the prospect of going anywhere near it. It might be telling your mother you won't be home for Christmas, a really important job interview, or asking your neighbours to turn the music down. Talk about these situations with someone you feel safe with, someone who already has some understanding of what assertiveness is about so that you can rehearse and role-play with them. It's important to run through the easy ones first and leave the emotionally-charged ones until you feel ready (which could be quite some weeks).

The assertiveness skill here is to be specific. This is the absolute bedrock, foundational skill on which all others are built, and which you can practise in all areas of your life, not just the difficult situations. Talk it through until you really know what it is you want and then practise saying the words that are right for you to say, rather than a parroted 'standard issue' sentence. What do you want? With the least difficult situations it should be something like: I want to take this skirt back to the shop and get a refund, or I want to tell my hairdresser not to cut the hair at my neck so short but to leave it an inch longer, or I want Sally to give me my CDs back, or I want Bill to put the milk bottle back in the fridge when he's done with it. Be this specific, make co-operation rather than confrontation your guiding intent, and the right words for you to say with genuine authenticity will emerge!

When I first did my own list of ten, my No.1 horror situation was the one I described earlier, the one which drove me on my search to the bookshop. What happened in the end? We never did become friends but because of the inner strength I found through understanding assertiveness, and the ability to use some of my new-found skills, I was no longer overwhelmed by fear in my encounters with my workmate. I have no idea whether she consciously made any changes in her own behaviour, but she definitely became less aggressive. I had the powerful realisation that she had to change because I changed, and so I was freed from the difficulty in our relationship. Free to relax and be really me!'

YOUR INNER VOICE

It's all very well talking about your voice and your message. But what does your voice say on the inside? There is the endless chatter that goes on inside your head morning until night. But have you ever stopped to think about what you're actually saying to yourself? Is it positive or negative? Is it empowering or disempowering? Does it make you feel good about yourself or chip away at your self-confidence?

When we look at presentation skills I will cover this in more detail, but the fact is that very often the negative messages running around your head like a tape playing can distract you from focusing on your message and delivery.

Do you get in your own way? Or to put it more clearly, do your own self-doubts and uncertainties hamper your journey? It's no good trying to convey a positive message if you've got negative messages on the inside.

How we see ourselves and what we say to ourselves can become a self-fulfilling prophecy. So it's back to basics.

You need to learn to walk your talk:
• Do as you say and lead by example.
• Believe in yourself (that really can't be down to anyone else).
• Fake it to make it.

However hard it is to be confident and clear, it is a process that can be learned and if we've spent most of our lives doubting ourselves and talking indirectly, then we need to start believing in ourselves and talking clearly. Even if we don't match the message we're hearing on the inside, believing 'as if' eventually synthesises with the message we're giving out. That's called 'faking it to make it.'

In other words, turn down the volume on the negative talk and turn the volume up on the positive. In the end we are the ones who choose what we listen to (like tuning in to a radio station of our choice) and we are also in control of what we want to say – even if it doesn't always feel like it.

PHYSICAL PROBLEMS

We've looked at different types of behaviour and how they can get in the way of using our voice powerfully and directly. But there's another aspect to this as well. And that's how not speaking our truth can affect us on the physical level – literally.

We all know those glib phrases like 'stuck in my throat', 'stiff upper lip' or 'through gritted teeth'. But they do have more serious meanings. When we talk about something being stuck in our throats we are usually referring to words that we want to say but somehow can't. Equally 'stiff upper lip' refers to powerful emotions that make our upper lip tremble. That can in turn refer to holding back our feelings or repressing them; it is the stiff upper lip that the English are so renowned for. What about 'feeling choked'? That's about holding back our feelings or words so they feel like they're strangling us. But the link between our emotions and our physical well-being is becoming a more widely accepted fact these days.

Louise Hay is an internationally renowned teacher and lecturer who has written many bestsellers, most notably *You Can Heal Your Life*. Based on her own experience of helping herself to overcome cancer through changing her mental thought patterns, she expounds the virtues of looking at the 'disease' in our life and the metaphysical causes of illness. We tend to think of disease as a physical problem. But try thinking of it as 'dis-ease' with oneself and one's emotions. Understanding our fears and resentments can have a profound effect on the rest of our lives. It is basically down to the link between cause and effect; if we look at the cause, we can start to change the effect or consequences of that cause.

Let's look at those physical symptom that affect our speech and our voice. According to holistic teachers, any kind of respiratory ailments are fundamentally to do with a fear of taking in life. It's back to the idea of breathing. Daring to breathe fully is about daring to live life fully; to speak our truth and not to be afraid of what others think of us.

- A sore throat may be about holding back anger and not feeling able to express our feelings truthfully. It may also represent an inability to move forward and accept change or stifled creativity.
- Stuttering may be linked with insecurity and a lack of self expression or not being able to cry.
- The root cause of tinnitus may be our refusal to listen or not listening to our inner voice.

The great thing about looking under the surface of life and its ailments is that there is often a direct correlation. Understanding what might be causing our problems is a major step towards solving them. Again it's down to taking responsibility for our lives.

Anne is a psychic in her sixties with excellent people skills. She is used to working with people on a one-to-one basis and just needed to brush up her presentation skills for working with a large audience. Here Anne talks about the power of our words and how vital it is to speak our truth.

'Our voice, our words, how we express ourselves and what we say are all so very important. We are sometimes afraid to speak our truth, to speak out or to speak up for ourselves. It starts in childhood when we are told 'little children should be seen and not heard'.

All my life, having had not only a Catholic upbringing, but a convent education to boot, I have suffered from the agony of being afraid to speak out. My work as a psychic is all about words. In the last decade or so I have extended my sphere of speaking to running workshops, courses and seminars. Quite a challenge; but what a great opportunity to stretch myself beyond my comfort zone!

Last year, I decided to run a large conference for hundreds of people. I wanted the day to be professional, slick, not the work of an 'amateur', so I rehearsed what I was going to say, tested the patience of all my family and friends by trying out my 'speeches' on them and got myself into a right old state with my efforts to put on a state-of-the-art performance. In the end, with some spiritual and worldly feedback, I got the message to just 'be myself, throw away the script and speak from the heart'.

It worked! For the first two minutes I was terrified as I looked down from the stage on the sea of faces. Then I remembered – I took a deep breath and just let my heart speak to the hearts of all who were there. The words flowed, the audience and I were one and the magic happened. The feedback was fantastic, with phone-calls, cards, letters, e-mails from those who were there to tell me how much they enjoyed the day and the miracles that happened for them. Not only did they all enjoy the day, but I did too!

The lesson I have learned is that our true power comes from authenticity. The authenticity of just being ourselves. Golda Meir once said something on the lines of 'If I am not myself, then who am I?' Our words and our speech are our power.'

We are what comes out of our mouths. A great teacher once said 'It is not what we put into our mouths that defines us, but what comes out of them'.

When we have throat problems, it may be because we are not speaking out or speaking our truth. It behoves us then to watch what we say, to speak kindly and non-judgementally, but to speak up, not to condone what we disagree with and always to speak from the heart. Our words have the power to harm or heal. Sometimes it takes 'tough love' to help someone. We so often do them a disservice by not saying what we think. And when we hold back our words we block our own power. Speak out. Speak your truth and speak with love; always speak with loving intent.

So the next time you feel like someone's strangled you or you suddenly lose your voice, ask yourself – what am I trying to avoid saying? Sometimes it doesn't even have to be verbalised. It's about being honest with yourself. Facing our own truths and realities can be a painful process. I believe we all know our own truth deep down and much of life's journey is about trying to find a way of expressing who we are and of being authentic.

VOICE AND COMMUNICATION

We've looked at ways of communicating, and will look at communication as a two-way process later on (p. 51–5). But how does that speaking out translate in terms of our voice?

Assertive Voice

This is when we are truly standing in our own power and speaking our truth. In other words, saying what we need to say, however difficult. If we sound convincing and sincere then the person on the receiving end is more likely to hear what we have to say.

Our facial expressions should reflect our message. So if we've got something positive and happy to say then we will smile and that smile will be reflected in our eyes and in our body. Our eyes will mirror our words, and our gestures will be open rather than closed.

In essence our voice, speech and expressions should match our message. If we feel, look and sound confident then the recipient will be left in no doubt that we mean what we say and, that in turn, will help them to respond in a positive, clear way.

If the saying 'what we give out we get back', is true, then the same goes for our voice. How we sound is often a reflection of how we feel. It's important to say at this point that in the early stages of working with assertiveness skills, you may not be feeling that confident because it's a new way of communicating. But like anything else, it's a learning curve and the more practice we have the better we'll get.

Aggressive voice

This is when we make our opinions into fact, bearing down on the unfortunate recipient in a threatening, aggressive manner. We can be quick to blame or be sarcastic. We don't listen to the other person because we're not interested in what they have to say. We are more than likely to step right into their body space and our voice is often loud and abrupt. We might be speaking very quickly, if only to stop the other person trying to get a word in edgeways. The eye contact will be intimidating and so will the body language, with no lots of pointing of fingers or crossed arms signalling defensive body language.

Passive voice

This is when someone sounds unsure about what they're saying: and let's face, it if they sound unsure then you are not going to be convinced by what they have to say. Telltale signs of someone who's feeling scared or nervous about the situation they're in is when their voice sounds high-pitched or there's no meaning in what they say. They speak in a dull, flat voice or just sound hesitant.

They will look nervous, perhaps looking away or down, which suggests that they are unsure about what they have to say and even more unsure that they're going to get the response they want. They might look like they're in some kind of pain as they clasp their hands or put their hand over their mouth. They're likely almost to apologise for what they have to say, as though they have no right to speak up.

VOICE AND EXPRESSION

Personality

We are all unique. That's possibly the most exciting and interesting thing about being human. There is only one of us. And our voice is a direct expression of who we are. These days we're encouraged to look at ourselves a little more deeply in order to be able to achieve our optimum in the world. It's no longer about trying to get better at the things you don't like doing but more about fulfilling your potential – in other words finding your voice in the world. And that starts with understanding who you are and where your strengths lie.

Just as we all have different voices, there are basic personality types. I like to think of a tribal connection. You walk into a group of people and you spot somebody across the room and they seem familiar to you. You know that you'll get on with them. They may remind you of someone else you know. They don't just look like that person physically but they seem to have the same characteristics. I found it fascinating when I did a lot of travelling at one point in my life to come across individuals I connected with who reminded me of other friends or relatives, despite the fact that they lived on the other side of the world.

There are lots of theories about personality types. The basic divide is between extrovert and introvert, but then you can subdivide these categories. We all have our individual DNA or blueprint which is what makes us unique and interesting – just as our voices can identify who we are. We might sound like someone else but there will be that unique quality to our voice which makes it our own. And if our voice reflects the essence of who we are, a contributing factor to that has to be our personality.

There are many other ways to define personality. Are you an optimist or a pessimist? Are you left-brained or right-brained? Research has shown that the brain can influence our personality and what we choose to do in life. If you work from the left-hand side of your brain, the theory goes, then you are a logical person who can analyse and think in a logical way. In fact your natural way of responding to a situation would be in a calculated and methodical one. If you're a right-brained thinker then you're more of an easy-going character who's likely to be seen as a creative type. You are imaginative and possibly a daydreamer. You could well be artistic or musically talented.

Carl Jung came up with another approach, the concept of the four basic natures of man. He argued that each human is born with a fundamental personality or way of operating, and divided us up into thinkers, feelers, intuiters and sensors, while recognising of course that these are simplifications and we are all multifaceted characters with other traits.

In the Jung classification, thinkers are those people who think logically and can work well with figures and facts and systems. Thinkers are more often than not extrovert, goal-orientated and good leaders. They're independently minded and less likely to worry about what other people think of them. They are usually confident and can be dynamic characters.

Those whose response system is via their feelings tend to be people-oriented and empathetic. They can almost feel the other person's emotions and they tend to be good communicators, coaches and counsellors. These types can be introverted because so much is going on inside. They can be inspiring and self-sacrificing.

We are all blessed with intuition. It's our inner alarm system and some schools of thought claim this should be our first response to any situation. What's your gut feeling? Even if everything on the outside is telling us to do something else, we may find our initial gut response is the one we should have listened to! Some people naturally work from their intuitive nature. It's not really something they have to develop. These types are often creative and ideas people. They can be visionaries.

Sensors are more practical, responsible, organising types. They make good communicators and can be focused and able to see things through. A sensor is someone who can put ideas into action. They are often good at negotiating deals because they are practical and down-to-earth.

Moods

It's not just our basic personality types that will affect how we communicate with others; how we are feeling and the mood we're in can have a tremendous impact on how we sound. If you're feeling low, deflated, lacking in energy, and you don't make an attempt to cover it up, then you're going to sound flat, down-in-the-mouth, uninterested. If things are going well and you are feeling optimistic, confident, happy, then undoubtedly that will have an impact on your communication with others.

Become aware of how you sound when you talk to other people. Do you sound enthusiastic, inspired and motivated? Or are you sounding like life's a total bore and you can't be bothered? Do you sound sad, despondent, scared, nervous, agitated?

23

It really isn't just about the words we say, it's much more about how we sound when we say it. When you have to ring a call centre how does that person respond when they pick up the phone? Do they make you feel valued as a customer and as though they care? Or do they sound indifferent and uninterested? How someone responds to us can make all the difference to how we respond to them.

We will look in more detail in a later chapter at situations in which we can improve our communication skills. Focusing on the voice now, imagine that each word we say has an emotion attached to it. If it doesn't, we come over as dull, monotonous and probably indifferent. If you are involved with what you are saying, then it will reflect in your message, its content and how it's received. In turn that can hugely influence the outcome you may want from a situation.

Let's look at different aspects of the voice and what we can do to make our message more resonant and meaningful.

Tone

Using our voice fully is about being able to totally express ourselves and allow feelings to come through. In my experience as a broadcaster and voice coach, tone is all-important. It gives the depth and resonance to a voice. I'm not talking about the sing-song voice we sometimes hear where the voice is going from high notes to lower notes in some kind of musical pattern, but when words are backed up with meaning.

I always believe that good voices are down to three things: preparation, focus and delivery. Preparation is thinking about who you are directing your message to, and it's also about the thought or intention we put into what we say. What are you saying and who are you saying it to? If you believe in what you say, so will the other person. Your belief will add weight to your tone of voice.

When you speak, always imagine that you are telling a story to one person. It doesn't matter if that one person is actually two hundred people in a conference room, because actually you want every individual to hear you and to feel as though you are talking to them personally.

This is particularly important if you are reading from a script. There's nothing worse than having an animated individual delivering their wise words and then reading something off a page that sounds utterly tedious and monotonous. It's about bringing your script or your story to life. Making it real and authentic. The tone of your voice is also about inflexion. Not just making the voice sound varied – as I mentioned before that just becomes a kind of 'sing-song' pattern – but using all of your voice so that your message is resonant and meaningful.

So how do you do that? Well, breathing properly is the first point; staying focused on your message and concentrating on what you're saying is the second; and don't lose the plot of the story. In other words, staying present and thinking about or even living the words you are saying will bring a natural resonance and meaning to what you're saying.

Over the years I have worked with media professionals and individuals from all walks of life and found that one of the best ways of getting someone to develop the tone of their voice is using news scripts. This is because in a short space of time you are telling a variety of stories, from tragedies to the humorous 'and finallys', and the only way you can get your viewer or listener to hear every word of every story is to keep them interested and to let them know each story is different.

If you read every story in the same tone of voice your audience will never know the difference between the sad story and the victorious football score in the sports bulletin. In fact, they'll probably get so bored with listening to a dull monotonous voice that they'll either switch channels or switch off! So it is the inflexion and meaning in your voice that will keep them hooked in. After all if you're not interested in what you're saying they certainly won't be!

Pace

It's easy to think that because we know what we're saying the other person will. But what if you're talking so quickly that they simply can't keep up? The added problem is that when we are faced with any kind of public speaking, presentation or interview, we are likely to automatically speed up through sheer nerves or tension.

It is important to consciously relax and slow down before attempting to say anything that's really important to you. There's no point in sabotaging the message by going onto fast forward without pausing. That will be a guarantee the recipient will not hear what you're saying. You will disconnect and all could well be lost!

The wonderful thing about good presentation and using your voice well is it's so simple. In fact the real problem is that it's too simple for us to get our heads round! You will be amazed to find how slowing down can make all the difference to your delivery and help you to keep in control of your message, rather than your message being in control of you.

Your pace will be naturally dictated by what you're saying. As long as you stay present and think about what you're saying (rather than how you're saying it or what you look or sound like!) then you will connect to a natural rhythm or pace.

I often train groups of police officers in media skills. The first part of the session involves taking them through the different types of media situations they're likely to face. I tend to relate my own experiences as a journalist and my relationships with the police. But talking virtually non-stop for an hour and attempting to be informative, entertaining, even amusing on occasions, is a challenge for lots of reasons. One is that I am trying to get some clear instructions across in an informative, entertaining way.

As soon as I get to the part about their presentation skills and how to give the best possible interview, the subject of pace inevitably comes up. And then, much to my embarrassment, I can hear how quickly I am talking! Just becoming aware of the pace I am going helps me to slow down and stay in touch with the message I am trying to give.

Exercise

This is something you can practise at any time. Just as you are probably becoming more conscious about your voice and how you use it, start listening to how fast you're talking. Whether it's in a business or social situation, self-monitoring is really useful! Are you gabbling or are you clear? Are you skimming or swallowing your words? If so, you are talking too quickly and not pausing for breath.

Pause

One of the most important words as far as improving your voice is concerned! The power of silence is extraordinary and can add volumes of depth and meaning to whatever you want to say.

Allowing your words to breathe helps the person who's listening to you digest what you're saying. That pause gets them to lean forward and listen a little closer! That pause can add drama to any tale you're telling. That pause helps them to integrate and absorb what you've said. It's also catch-up time for you to take a much needed breath and it allows natural and necessary spaces in your story.

Volume

If we have to divide people into categories, I guess it's fair to say there are loud people and quiet people. Outgoing and shy. Extrovert and introvert. And as discussed their voice will often reflect the kind of person they are. A bit like that first handshake; we will come on to body language in a later chapter. So some people are naturally quieter than others.

Regardless of how quiet or loud you are, it's important to use the full range of your voice; the full palette of colours. But you also need to be aware of the volume of your voice. Being heard is not about shouting. If you shout, you will more than likely be using the top part of your body rather than speaking from the stomach. This will make you sound high-pitched and, for women, perhaps even squeaky, and you will end up exhausted. You should really be speaking from the central part of yourself, your stomach. This not only helps your voice to sound resonant and rich but also helps with volume control.

Of course breathing properly is central to this. The more air you have, the better your voice.

Exercise

Using visual images can be effective for improving your voice. One of the ones I use in coaching sessions is that of a tape recorder – not quite obsolete yet in these days of high-tech equipment! Imagine you have a large volume control, and when you want to turn up the volume of your voice or turn it down, use the volume control.

Again, if you are mindful of the content of what you're saying, you will naturally have the right tone and colour in your voice and it will be quite apparent as to how loud and soft your voice should be. Just as you have top notes and low notes, you need to have louder notes and soft notes – not to mention all the ones in between. Think of a keyboard and make sure you not only know all the notes on it but include them in your repertoire.

I love listening to the speaking voice. Listening to a piece of prose being read by a wonderful voice is like listening to good music. The voice can soothe and heal or it can jar and destroy. Our voice is the mouthpiece of who we are. And remember you never have a second chance to make a first impression and the same goes for your voice.

There is no doubt that we are judged on how we speak. It's not about accents. They're positively in vogue these days and it's the non-accented broadcaster who's more likely to have problems getting the job! But it is about the depth and range of our voice.

Close your eyes and listen to a reading of a favourite work, whether Shakespeare or Kahil Gibran. Read well, it can completely alter your mood. That is the power of the voice. Remember you don't have to a famous actor or broad-caster to make a big difference. You want people to remember you, to identify you, and your voice is one of the best ways to achieve that.

Another great way to practise using your full voice is to read to children. If you have kids then you will know exactly what I mean. It's easier to lose our inhibitions and to drop into the role of wicked witch or fairy queen. That shared experience is not only great for bonding the adult and child but it's fantastic practise for you and your voice. It helps, of course, to find a story that you're reasonably interested, in as opposed to something that bored you rigid as a child and still does as an adult. Find a descriptive book with language you enjoy – or a favourite poem – and give it a go. You could well be surprised at what you hear back.

Your barometer as to how you're doing will come from your audience. If the child is looking enraptured and entranced and hanging on your every word, then you've hit the mark. It's a good way also of overcoming your own shyness with your voice. It's such an intimate part of ourselves that we have to learn to get to know our voice and its depth and range. But because we might be a bit shy of revealing it, we need a safe place to explore it.

Again storytelling to children is a great way of doing that. Storytelling as an art has been around for centuries. It's interesting that in these days of state-of-the-art technology there are still many storytellers around the world capturing large audiences who want to listen to tales of old – the myths and the fairy tales that they heard as a child and tell to their children today.

In fact next time you hear someone reading a story, whether it's on the radio or in a kids' classroom, listen to how they *tell* the story. Pick up some tips. What did you enjoy about the performance or what didn't you like?

Remember – don't be daunted by the prospect of thousands of television viewers or an audience of hundreds. In essence we are always telling a story to one person at a time.

2. AUDIENCE
Who Are You Talking to?

It is perhaps debatable as to which comes first, who you are addressing or what you are going to say. Both are equally important, but knowing who you are talking to is fundamental in constructing your message. Whatever the situation your audience is critical. Whether you are trying to get your pupil to listen to you in class or hold a wedding audience rapt, you are halfway there if you have given some thought and consideration to who is actually listening to you. Or perhaps I should say, how are you going to get them to listen to you in the first place?

How you might address guests at a family celebration will be different from how you might address a business audience. Sounds obvious, but most of the problems we may encounter in presentation and communication come from ignoring the basics. One of those basics is having a plan. Preparation is at least 50 per cent of a good presentation.

Fundamental to a good presentation is engaging your audience. You have to think about how to address them. Think carefully about who you are talking to. Knowing your audience is a key factor in preparing what you're going to say and the language you use. To be effective you need to do your research. You have to make your speech, presentation or interview relevant to the people who are going to listen to you.

Let's take the police as an example. These days they are more determined than ever to be accountable to the public and also they depend on us civilians to help them solve their crimes. Whenever they put out an appeal to the public, they are relying on at least some of us to be able to give them information that in turn will help them arrest someone or help prevent similar incidents.

When I do media training sessions with the police, I always tackle first the problem of 'police speak' and try to persuade them to talk conversationally. Secondly they need to be aware of exactly who they are targeting their message at. For example if they are trying to warn young girls and women not to walk alone at night because there's a rapist on the loose, they have to ensure they catch the attention of the female population. So they have to address parents and women directly in their message. If they're looking at crimes against the elderly, then they have to consider where to place their prevention message. Choosing a young person's radio station is not necessarily going to work! The radio station which they know the older person in the community is more likely to listen to is the obvious choice.

The other point about the audience is that they are hearing our story or message for the first time. So however much we know about a particular subject, we must remember that our audience (and that could be just one person or hundreds) have never heard it before.

So on all counts don't make assumptions. You need to consider the expectations of your audience. How much do they know in general about the subject? These kind of considerations will also help later with the planning of your message. Is your audience there by choice or because they've been told to go along and listen to you? Whatever the reasons, you need to be confident that you are going to fulfil their expectations.

At the very beginning of your speech you need to convince your audience that they will get something positive out of listening to you. You need to hook them in from the start of your story to the very end.

I recently heard a voice expert saying that presentations of any kind were like storytelling. I agreed with that bit of his argument. We are always telling a story to one person. But I tend to disagree with what he went on to say, which is that like a story you should start off slowly and build up to an exciting or positive crescendo at the end of the story.

As a journalist I was taught 'hook them in from the start' – and keep them hooked whatever it takes. I have found this method works in presentations as well. But you can only deliver a stimulating and informative address if you have researched your audience and know the kind of content they are going to be interested in.

AUDIENCE RESEARCH

You have to do your research whoever you are addressing and in whatever setting. First of all you need to know:

- Who is going to be there.
- Why they are there.
- What their expectations are.
- What they want to go away with.

Is it formal or informal, social or business? And what will they know about you and what you are going to say? It is almost impossible to pitch your message correctly if you don't know what it's all about. You can never ask too many questions, particularly if it's going to spare you some embarrassment and awkwardness on the day.

The advantages of one-to-one situations or small audiences is that you can include them in a more personal way. It is easier for the participants to feel they can ask questions or get you to retrace something you've said than if they are in a larger audience. When the audience gets larger it is down to you as the facilitator or presenter to gauge how your listeners are responding to you. If, for example, you think they may have misunderstood something then you can reiterate whatever section you need to, saying something like: 'Just to clarify…'

TYPES OF AUDIENCE

One-to-one

Continuing with my favourite theme of this book! Remember that in a sense you are always talking to one person at any time. In other words your story, speech, address or interview has to interest each and every person – or even the one person – you're talking to. It can be daunting enough talking to one person if you have something important to say, so thinking it through beforehand is vital to your delivery.

But if we envisage ourselves as always talking just to one person, that can help to ease the nerves and make us more relaxed and comfortable. Imagine you are in a conversation with someone where you are so engrossed in what you're saying that you don't worry about your content and delivery, it comes naturally.

That's because you're present in the conversation. You are thinking about what you're saying and not how you're saying it. Keeping connected is the key. So when you're faced with a group or large audience it's worth remembering that really you're talking to one person at a time. You want each and every person to feel that you are speaking to them, so they feel included.

A current trend in the media is to get journalists or correspondents to talk to the presenter in very personal terms. So, for example, when the presenter intro-duces them he or she might say, 'Well, Robert, what's happening?' They in turn will say, 'Well, Jane…' and often continue to address Jane as though she was the only person listening to them. In both radio and television terms, I believe this can leave the listener or viewer feeling they've been excluded from the conversation. Equally when contributors start ingratiating themselves with the presenter, what happens to us individuals tuned in at home?

It is vital that we include our audience, whether it's one person, a hundred, or even thousands!

Business

Naturally the setting or context in which our message is delivered is a major factor. This brings up an important point. Is your audience there because their boss told them to go or are they generally there by choice? Willing and reluctant participants can make a difference in the planning! Are you talking about a subject that your audience knows something or nothing about? Are they likely to be for you, against you or relatively indifferent? Like any kind of sales pitch, you have to get your audience interested and wanting more information. But how you do that depends on the research you've done beforehand.

If it's a business subject that your audience knows something about, then obviously you have to ensure that what you're telling them is new and informative – or dress some old facts in new clothes! When it comes to the commercial world there are generally some key factors to consider, such as rewards, prospects, job satisfaction, motivation, time management, etc.

We will look at the content side of presentations in the next chapter, on Message, but you can't begin to do that until you know who your audience are, what they already know and what their expectations might be.

Above all else you must enjoy what you have to say. Once you've planned and thought through relevant points and stories that are going to engage your audience, with some humorous anecdotes or the odd joke thrown in for good measure, you want them to feel as though you are glad to be spending that time with them.

One person who's used to addressing all types of audiences, large and small, is Steve Egginton. A newspaper and broadcast journalist, who has been head of radio and television newsrooms up and down the country and is now Head of News and Sport at ITV West, he's turned speech-making into something of an art form. Here's how:

'I was once asked to address a Rotary Club in the depths of Wiltshire on a miserable winter's night and every single member turned up – all 12 of them. My reward was a free plate of curry and chips and a couple of contacts who have kept me supplied with stories ever since. So whether you are hungry for tip-offs, or just plain hungry, public speaking can have its rewards, most obviously the chance to spread the word about you and your organisation. And if you are any good, and word goes round, you could have a meal-ticket for life, since finding the weekly speaker is the bane of every social secretary's job.

On another occasion, I was asked to address a Women's Institute in the middle of the Forest of Dean. When I told them I had once lived in Sling, right in the middle of the Forest, I was adopted en masse as their grandson. When I told them I had my Fern Token with me, there was a lot of laughter and spilt tea. More on that later.

Public speaking wasn't something I ever set out to do, but it seemed to come with the job, especially as I climbed the management ladder. You obviously reach your audience through the bit of paper or wire that you work on, but personal contact also matters.

And no two meetings are ever quite the same.

The most extreme case came in Oxford where I faced a crowd of brolly-waving protesters, who didn't like some of the changes being made to their local radio station. I invited them in out of the rain, talked to them for an hour, gave them lots of literature and goodies, and promised to listen to their concerns. All agreed it was an honourable draw – and I got loads of publicity in the local paper.

But that's unusual. We are more concerned here with the formal invitation that asks you to address a public gathering. It can be a daunting challenge, especially having to sit there sober, while everybody else gets hammered, until they are ready for you to perform. And then if you bore them, they will start heckling, or simply resume the conversation they were already enjoying with their mates over the brandy and cigars.

So the first rule has to be: know your audience and adapt your speech accordingly. Are they are a bunch of old chaps who are simply pushed out from under the wife's feet for a couple of hours a week, or professionals with a keen interest in the subject matter?

I think it helps to start off by telling them a bit about yourself, so they can start to relate to you, before you get into the nitty gritty of the talk. Do some homework, so you know a bit about the organisation, or the locality where you are speaking. Try to pick up a couple of anecdotes about the group or individuals in the audience. I remember talking to a Chamber of Commerce in Somerset and being told a couple of the members might be late because they had been celebrating until the wee small hours. When they appeared, ten minutes into my talk, I left a pregnant pause before enquiring politely how their heads felt this morning.

Try and engage the audience – do they read your newspaper or watch your television programme – and if not why not? And always leave time for questions. Intersperse the facts and figures you want to get across, with the odd story or joke. They love to hear tales out of school – what such and such a columnist or presenter is really like, what it was like to cover the Concorde crash, or some other big story.

But tailor the talk to suit them. The local Rotary probably had a talk about Derek's recent holiday to Papua, New Guinea, last week, so anything you can give them is likely to be a treat. And although we get cynical and blasé about it, working in any branch of the media is perceived to be glamorous. They want to hear the nuts and bolts of what you do, but beware of jargon – though 'cock-up' is an old printing expression and perfectly acceptable!

For informal talks like this, don't use PowerPoint or other gadgets, which will always refuse to work and might send them to sleep anyway. Keep it short and punchy; most of them will probably have to leave at 2pm, either to go back to work or have their afternoon nap. And if you can leave them laughing, by playing a bloopers tape, for example, so much the better.

Even with more formal affairs, I think the same basic pattern applies, though you might need technical aids to get the facts across. And take plenty of business cards.

After-dinner speaking is a completely different world, where high-quality speakers can command big fees, so maybe that's something I should aspire to. When I have done them I have had to revise my repertoire of jokes and stories. I think it's called dumbing down.

But the all-purpose parrot joke is OK for the average daytime audience. A man goes into a shop to find an array of parrots, all with different qualifications, and a rising scale of value. You can be as silly and as protracted as you like with this section, but you can adapt the punchline to suit the audience. So when I told it to colleagues from the BBC, it went like this. Customer: 'This parrot's the most expensive in the shop. What can he possibly do to be worth so much?' Reply: 'No-one's seen this parrot do anything, but the others all call him Director General.'

So back to the ladies of the WI and the Fern Token, as related to me by the Rev. Geoffrey Crago, a fine broadcaster, who was told he had earned his Fern Token after being the incumbent in the parish of Drybrook, deep in the Forest of Dean, for some time. Geoffrey naturally assumed this was some ancient Forest honour, born Tyme Out Of Mind, as they say over there, and that he had finally been accepted by the

Foresters. When he asked about its significance he was told: 'The Token entitles the holder to roll the Forest girls in the ferns!'

Good night!'

Social

The idea of speaking on a family occasion or in front of a group of friends might sound easier than standing up at a business presentation, but it can be even more intimidating talking to people you know well.

I had been used to broadcasting and interviewing and speaking in public for many years. But I can safely say the most nerve-racking experience I had was when I was invited to one of my children's school fund-raising evenings to give a talk on good communication skills.

I had to speak after a nationally renowned chef who gave a wonderful demonstration on how to make soufflés and delicious puddings, which were duly sampled by the large and impressed audience in the school hall. It was a hard act to follow! I found myself, armed with my trusty tape recorder, looking at a sea of faces which included friends who had earlier commiserated about how difficult a task I faced!

I attempted to hide my ever-increasing nerves by doing a practical exercise which involved hauling up a reluctant member of the audience to give a 'before and after' demonstration on voice training. It would have gone well if my tape recorder hadn't packed up in the middle. I smiled and battled on, trying to ensure that I stayed with my message rather than listening to the negative self-talk going on in my head.

It all passed in a bit of a blur. But amazingly the audience seemed to have enjoyed the session and said they found the practical tips useful. Perhaps they could relate to the humanness of the situation and sympathised with me. I realised later that one of the assumptions I make about any audience I work with, small or large, is that they probably know everything I'm telling them anyway. I've discovered that, even if this is the case, reminding them about the basics is helpful, and as long as I come over as genuine and I target my message then I can't go far wrong. And when it doesn't go according to plan, then a sense of humour is essential!

For some people the idea of talking to a large audience can seem a piece of cake compared to smaller groups or even social occasions. Alan is an IT manager:

'As the manager of a busy IT department I was often called on to give presentations to all sorts of people. The audiences ranged from the senior management team to completely external groups. It really didn't matter. I enjoyed making presentations and I'd been told many times that I was good at it. So it would have been perfectly natural to assume that I was equally at home speaking out in meetings, networking at conferences, and going to parties. But I wasn't. My boss thought I was too quiet in meetings, and I'd always found it difficult to start a conversation with people I didn't know, whether it was a business event or a social one. Sometimes I'd even find it difficult to break into a conversation with people I did know. Something had to change, so I went to Joanna to find out why my presentation skills and confidence didn't carry over into the other aspects of my life.

I thought the problem was that I was softly spoken and that, because I've never really liked the sound of my voice, I was self-conscious. That was why I preferred to listen, rather than talk, and why I usually waited for someone to ask me a question before I joined the conversation. I expected Joanna to help me develop my voice so that I could speak up without shouting, and give it presence. And she did, but that wasn't the main problem because, obviously, I could do all of that when I was presenting. Joanna thought that my problem was that I was always waiting for someone to give me permission to speak! Whenever I gave a presentation it was because I had been asked to give it whereas, for the rest of my working life, I had always been the IT expert sitting quietly in the corner and waiting for someone to ask for my expertise.

Joanna's solution was to find ways to give myself 'permission to speak', which she did by showing me how to use my posture, breathing, and my voice, to join a conversation when I wanted to, not when someone else asked me to. In effect, she took all of the things that I did automatically whenever I stood up to present, and showed me how to do them sitting down. The sceptical side of me said it couldn't be this easy.

One day later my wife and I were due to have dinner with some good friends we hadn't seen for a while. We thought that it would just be the four of us and a chance to catch up with each other, but we quickly discovered that we were part of a larger dinner party and we only knew the hosts. Normally I would have gone into my attentive listener mode but, fresh from my day with Joanna, I tried the techniques we had been talking about and dived into the conversation. It worked! In fact it worked so well that when we got to the car at the end of the evening my wife asked what had happened to her normally quiet husband. She knew, of course, but she liked the change.

A few days later I had another opportunity to practise my new skills at a meeting in London with a small group of my peers. I had attended this group before and would normally have been content to sit back and wait for someone to ask me for my opinion. But not this time. Using Joanna's hints and tips on presence I started to make the points that I wanted to make when I wanted to make them. A few weeks later I was able to practise my new skills again at an IT Directors' Forum. This was an event where I had previously been content to listen during the seminars, and where I had struggled to make small talk over dinner, so there were lots of opportunities to practise my new skills. And to good effect, as I got a lot more out of the event this year.

But the technique didn't always quite so smoothly. At another meeting in London, again with a number of my peers from other organisations, I was keen to contribute my ideas to the formation of a new group. But try as I might, I couldn't break into the debate. This was partly due to poor facilitation but largely due to the fact that a few very powerful speakers were just talking over each other to make their points and I wasn't comfortable doing that.

By the middle of the meeting I still hadn't managed to break into the flow of suggestions, and I was both annoyed at myself for failing to do so and disappointed to realise that any comment I did make at that stage would be lost in the general melée. The old me would have just gone into listener mode, but the new me did not want to have to admit that to Joanna next time I saw her. So I decided to wait until the end of the meeting, then deliberately break in (no matter how) by offering a summary of the key points discussed so far and adding my ideas to the list at that point. In the end I needed to talk over someone to do it, which was a new experience for me, but I did. And I felt good about doing it. I felt even better when the founder of the group spoke up to say that he thought that the ideas were really good!'

So as Alan's story shows, it's really all about inner confidence. Daring to take the risk and have a go. And as he proved, the rewards are great!

SUMMARY

Whoever your audience is they have expectations of some kind of another. First you have to consider the following points.

- Who are you talking to?
- What are you talking about?
- What will your audience learn from your talk/address?
- What are they going to be doing during the talk – is it formal or informal?
- Will they need to take any notes or will you be giving handouts?
- What do they want from this talk?
- Are they here by choice or are they listening to you because someone else has told them to?

3. MESSAGE
What Are You Saying?

The first two chapters have looked at how to use your voice to best effect in all kinds of communication, both professional and social, and how to tailor that communication to the audience you are addressing, whether it's an audience of one or of thousands. So what are you trying to say? It seems so simple that we sometimes overlook the importance or thinking through and planning our message. One of the great myths is that we have to wow our audience with clever words or funny jokes.

The fact is that in most situations we are telling a story and we want to keep our audience interested. How do we do that? We do it by targeting the audience that we have identified with a message that is going to hold their attention. In this chapter we are going to explore the content and format of the message you are giving.

PLANNING YOUR MESSAGE

Once you've established who it is you are talking to, you have to consider how to keep them interested. Your goal is to keep them hooked in from start to finish; and more than that, you want them to take something with them when they go. What can you give them or tell them that at best could be life-changing, or at least memorable?

If it's a subject that they know something about, then the goal will perhaps be to give them markers to familiar material, but also additional information that will either challenge their existing beliefs or help them to achieve a wider perspective. You are not necessarily there to make them feel comfortable. You never know how that one piece of challenging information may change someone's life for ever by giving them choices they didn't know they had before or moving them to a new level of awareness.

But remember that just because you know all about what you want to say doesn't mean that your audience will be familiar with it. One of the key factors to be aware of is that, more than likely, you are giving our audience information they haven't heard before. It's back to basics then: those reminders are going to be helpful anyway.

Often when I am doing voice coaching-sessions with people and seem to point out the obvious, they are quite cross with themselves that they had not seen it for themselves. But that's the problem - we generally try to complicate what we say and forget that keeping it simple is often the most powerful and profound message we can give people.

So how do you go about identifying your own goals and objectives? Sometimes the very idea of a speech or presentation or media interview is so overwhelming it can feel hard to get past the fear stage! But the bottom line is that you know more about the subject matter than your audience. So you can rule that fear out first of all. It's more likely that you have too much information about your subject and will need to edit it. Don't forget that you have something important to offer. Something of value that will be appreciated by your audience, whether of one or a hundred. If you start the process by feeling that kind of confidence it will in turn help you to feel inspired and motivated.

Sometimes we can waste a great deal of time sitting behind a computer screen wondering what we're going to write – or what we're going to say. Just as preparation is a key word in the actual presentation process, so is preparation in the initial stages. Before you commit anything to paper or screen, allow your creative processes to get up and running.

How might you do that? Go for a walk in the countryside. Listen to your favourite piece of music. Isn't baroque music meant to get our creative brain in gear? Personally, I have found that going for a swim and thinking about nothing more than the number of lengths I have done has been very helpful with some of the more creative projects I have worked on. Just as I reach length 32, a thought pops into my head and it's fundamental to the book I'm writing or the presentation I am preparing.

It's as if giving our brains a rest allows other more creative thoughts to come into our awareness. And frankly it just doesn't matter how you get there. Any route is fine as long it works for you. What do you enjoy doing? Allow what personally inspires you in life to inspire you in your speech or presentation. Remember in the end it's what you bring to the stage or the audience. It's part of your spirit and essence.

What is it that inspires you in others? Who is your favourite actor or performer? Often it is their uniqueness that is so attractive. Their ability to bring part of themselves onto the stage or screen. It's their talent to make words come alive and to include you in that process.

Just as you aim to enrich and enliven your audience, so you need also to bring inspiration to what you're saying. Inevitably that means you have to be inspired from the start of the process yourself. If you're bored with the whole concept there is absolutely no chance you're going to interest anyone else.

There's a mistaken belief that you should only spout external knowledge and not make any personal references. That's simply not true. If you have a valid anecdote or example to back up a point you are making, then use it. It brings meaning to what you're saying and adds a reality check.

Your audience doesn't just want to hear a whole load of facts and figures. They'd much rather the statistics were brought to life with a relevant story and some human interest. How often have you warmed to someone once they've trusted you enough to reveal more of themselves?

Inspiration is one of the keys to creating and conveying a good, effective message. Whatever your preconceived notions about yourself, anyone can be creative and inspired – it's just finding the route that suits you. Are you left-brained or right-brained? Do you tend to think logically or creatively? We are all unique and wired differently. It helps to make the world a more interesting place! On that basis there's no right or wrong way to discover your inner potential; it's just finding the right way for you.

If your mind has gone a complete blank at the thought of the particular message you want to give, that's just anxiety! Take a deep breath and remember you do know what you're talking about, otherwise you wouldn't have been the one chosen to come up with the speech or presentation. And here are a couple of useful techniques to get your mind working creatively.

Mind-mapping

If you do need to generate some ideas, one way to go about it is to mind map. This is a technique developed by Tony Buzan and described in his many publications. He wanted to discover a memory system and came up with one based on the Ancient Greek principles of Imagination and Association. He also noticed how people often doodled when they were thinking about things or trying to brainstorm ideas. Hence the notion of mind-mapping. Tony Buzan – who's now a best selling-author worldwide – calls it the ultimate organisational thinking tool.

And the wonderful thing about it is it's simple and fun. Anyone can use this system, from kids to adults and in any walk of life. It's note-taking with a difference; all you need is a blank sheet of paper and some coloured pens or crayons. You put your central subject in the middle of your page and draw roads leading out from the centre, each with an image or word that will help you to work on your speech; like branches on a tree with lots of twigs representing points you want to make. You can use words, symbols or both. According to Tony Buzan, who has become so successful through creating this method that he advises international athletes, major companies and governments, the rule is one key word or image for one minute's worth of speech on a topic that you know well.

The ultimate goal is to give you an overall picture of the situation, or in this case the speech you are going to make. It's a fun and effective way of preparation and can make the planning part of the process much more enjoyable and creative.

Brainstorming

Brainstorming is really a form of free association. You think of a word and then come up with other words and ideas that are inspired by that original word. Don't be daunted. This is probably taking you back to childhood - you might have played the game where one person thinks of a word and the next person thinks up another word that has some association with it. If there's a group of people it can be quite fascinating to see where it can go.

For example, if you came up with the word 'speech' you could come up with many associated words such as – words, content, audience, subject matter, nervous, voice, cough, cold, flu, illness, doctor, medicine and so on! Have a go at using the subject-matter you're working with. Come up with the core word and write down anything that comes into your mind and you will be amazed at the results and how creative this process can be.

STRUCTURING YOUR MESSAGE

Once you've got your basic ideas together, it's helpful to put a frame around what you are going to say. How are you going to approach the subject-matter? What's your goal and how can you best get your message across?

Framing is putting a boundary around your presentation: what you put in and, just as importantly, what you leave out. A frame leads the eye into the picture that it surrounds. A framework around your speech draws the audience in to focus on your conversation or presentation.

Framing is a like an editing process but you do it before you have come up with the final content rather than afterwards. What fits into the frame and what doesn't? You should consider whether you are:

- Recounting personal experiences (like an after-dinner speaker)
- Presenting a problem and coming up with possible solutions
- Telling a story
- Persuading them
- Presenting the 'for' and 'against'

One of the most useful things that I was told as a journalist when I set out on my life in the media was to think of every story as a pyramid. What's the most important point you want to make? What's the second most important point, third most important, and so on. Once you get to the bottom of the pyramid, you have expanded your story out and you are filling in more detail but you have managed to get the most salient points in at the top.

Trainee journalists, or anyone being introduced to the media, will usually be told that a story is made up of answers to the following questions:
- Who
- Why
- What
- When
- Where
- How

One training organisation I work for use the phrase 'TED':
- Tell me
- Explain to me
- Describe for me

Whatever format or order you choose to present in, it is important to be fair and balanced. Remember you can't please all of the people all of the time. If you want to make a controversial point then obviously not everyone's going to agree with you. You have to constantly hold the overview. This is different from illustrating a point with a personal story.

Presenting a reasoned argument is more likely to get the winners on your side.

We will be looking at the language and the skills needed to construct your presentation and report in the next few chapters; at this stage we are still looking at the content and the format. Deciding the framework or format you are going to use is one of the first steps. Let's look at some examples.

1. *For and against debate*
   Here you need to present the overall picture before pitching reasons for and against the issue. Once you've given a fair and balanced argument, you need to summarise and end with some clear pointers, just as a judge would sum up a trial. Then the members of the jury, or the audience in your case, have to go away and consider their verdict.

2. *Storytelling*
   As with all stories, each has its own individual flavour and narrative. You can either start with a dramatic hard-hitting introduction and try to sustain that level of interest throughout the narrative. Or you can start slowly, easing the audience in and building up to the dramatic conclusion, which may be a cliff hanger, a happy or sad ending, or one which leaves your audience with something to go away and think about.
      Storytelling is becoming increasingly popular in the workplace as well as the classroom. It's an effective technique for presenting ideas in a creative, inspiring way that the audience will be able to relate to.

3. *Report*
   Reports by their very nature can be boring and something of a turn-off. So even if you are confronted with the task of presenting a long-winded report to your colleagues, why not make it relevant and interesting? There is absolutely no reason why some dull statistics can't be dressed up with some engaging examples. Just as a newspaper tells you the story in a few, simple paragraphs, you should try to simplify your report. Don't blind the audience with a pile of irrelevant facts and stats that will make them blank out. Give them a couple of mindblowing figures and some relevant stories and you can keep them hooked from start to finish.

4. *Topical/pyramid structure*

This is where you are going to concentrate on the who, what, why, when, where at the top of your story. It's putting the hard-hitting facts first and expanding your story and detail as it progresses. This format can work well if you have to précis your information.

5. *Chronological structure*

As you would expect, this approach chronicles your subject-matter. So if you were taking your audience through stages you could use a chronological structure. This can be helpful if you are showing the development of a product or person and by its very logic helps to construct a framework for your topic.

6. *Spatial structure*

You are more likely to use this type of structure in a cultural context. You can divide your presentation up into counties, towns and districts, or countries and continents. Again this is a clear and easy framework to use, given the right subject-matter.

7. *Illustrative/practical*

This is when you pepper your talk or speech with real life examples – and have to stop worrying that your audience don't want to know anything about you! They do! Personalising your presentation can bring your subject-matter to life, endear you to your audience and help them to identify with what you're saying. It works particularly well if you can tell a story against yourself.

Needless to say I have plenty of these kind of anecdotes up my sleeve! One of my best is to tell the story of how not to get misquoted in a newspaper.

Despite being a journalist for nearly three decades and a well-established media trainer, I once made the fatal mistake of giving an interview to a tabloid hack over the telephone. It was about a controversial subject of which I had some experience and I was assured I would be represented in the best possible light.

I was circumspect in my answers and I believe realistic. The biggest mistake I made was believing the reporter in the first place and letting my three children answer her questions down the phone with yes and no responses. A grave error, as you will learn in the chapter on media skills. What they were in fact saying yes and no to were the reporter's biased questions which she was then able to turn into a direct quote – or not.

When the paper came out I was utterly devastated to discover that the story completely misrepresented me and my family, and all the quotes had been changed or manipulated to tell the story the paper wanted rather than the one I had actually told. There was nothing I could do except wait for the letters of complaint or to be sued by someone! It was actually a traumatic experience and taught me a great deal about what it's like to be on the other side of the fence and to suffer the dreadful injustice of being misquoted and misrepresented. I hope I am a better journalist and trainer as a result of that experience!

But the real point of this anecdote is that it always goes down well with the groups to whom I teach media training skills. It shows that dog really does eat dog and that we have to take personal responsibility for any situation that we get ourselves into!

RESEARCHING YOUR MESSAGE

Once you have come up with the topic you're going to talk about, then you have to make sure you've got the material and facts to back up what you're saying. Obviously if it's a subject you know a great deal about, then you will have your own research material, but if some of it is an unknown quantity then you have to access material from various sources.

Don't overlook family and friends as a first point of contact for any information you may need. Next stop the workplace? You never know what kind of strange of interesting things your colleagues may be up to. It could be the shy person in the corner who has an extraordinary leisure pursuit or who knows all about the subject-matter you've got to talk about!

Next there's always the library or local business centre. If I wasn't such a technophobe my first point of reference would of course be the internet – a world-wide library at the touch of a button.

So do not be daunted if there are some facts and figures you need to find; they may well be more accessible than you would imagine.

It might be useful at this stage to warn of some pitfalls to avoid. Always useful to look at these in the early stages rather than committing them on the night!

The first is to not put yourself in a position of authority, nor see being on the podium as a chance to lecture (in the worst sense of the word), moralise, patronise, judge, condemn, label, psychoanalyse or command.

Second, be sensitive to your audience's sensitivities. You can never be one hundred per cent sure who's in your audience or who you could offend inadvertently. The obvious areas to watch out for are racial and religious issues and, as a general rule, politics is often a good subject to avoid!

In this vital preparation stage, try to discover what your audience is expecting from you; do some discreet research with the organisers and check if there any sensitive issues to skirt. You don't want to start making jokes about extra-marital or office affairs and discover later that the MD is having a discreet liaison with his PA. You probably won't be asked back!

This brings me neatly onto the subject of language. Often it's not what we say but how we say it that makes a speech memorable or infamous.

EXPRESSING YOUR MESSAGE

There is no doubt that words have power. In this book I also want to argue that the way in which we say words is critical. How we say something can make all the difference to how our message is received, and we can help our delivery enormously by thinking about how we are going to say something.

One of the greatest skills of the journalist is to reduce a long and rambling story to a few concise and clear paragraphs. While we may all have something to say about the tabloid newspapers, one thing's for sure – the writing is clear and direct, and you are left in no doubt as to what the story is.

It is a myth to think that using too many words or sounding like you've read *Roget's Thesaurus* from cover to cover is going to impress your audience. Believe me, less is more. It's not just your tone of voice, it's the impression that the words you use give. For example do you sound tired and weary of your subject, are you excited and challenged, are you motivated, sad, angry, irritated, confusing or clear? You can totally influence your audience by the words you use and the type of message you're giving them.

How many times have we been wounded or confused by something someone's said to us? Often we've picked up completely the wrong message because of the way it's been delivered.

So when you're giving a speech or a presentation you cannot afford to give the wrong impression to your audience. After all, you never get a second chance to make a first impression. Try to choose positive words rather than negative words. The rule to live by when it comes to script writing is – minimum script, maximum delivery.

According to the *The Complete Idiot's Guide to Clear Communication*, by Kris Cole, the 500 most commonly used words in the English language have an average of 28 meanings each. That astounding fact leads me to another important point to make. We, as the scriptwriters and speechmakers, have to be sure what we are saying. Once we know what our intention is then, like a sharpened arrowhead, it's going to get the message cleanly across to the audience.

As we've already discussed, how we say something and the way in which we say it is vital, but one of the foundation stones has to be the script. The planning, preparation and writing.

If at any point you say something that could confuse your audience then you stand a good chance of losing them. They'll be so busy wondering what you were trying to say that they'll disconnect from the other pearls of wisdom that you're spouting. Back to the maxim, less is more. When it comes to talking it's no good trying to be clever or superior by using language that will not only make you seem pompous and arrogant but will no doubt leave your audience stranded.

There can be a great danger of trying to impress your colleagues or peer group and forgetting entirely who you are addressing your message too.

I was once asked to give a talk to some anaesthetists about how to talk to the media. One of the messages was about remembering that they were in all probability going to to be talking to people who were potential hospital patients and that it was very important to use language they would be reassured rather than frightened by. Many people can be positively phobic about hospitals or even the medical profession because it's not often that we're going to visit them for good news!

At the end of the lecture one of the anaesthetists stood up and said she couldn't possibly use conversational words because what would her medical professors think! We had an interesting discussion and I have to say it took some persuading to get her to realise that the only person who matters when you deliver your message is the person or people you are addressing!

In the end you don't sound at all clever when the intended audience doesn't understand what you're saying and the person you're trying to impress isn't even listening because they're not actually your target audience.

It doesn't matter what profession you're in, the same basic rules apply. I know as a journalist that we unintentionally tend to view our audience as the other journalists we work with – who are also of course our rivals. As you know it's all about getting the story first and beating the competitor. But the person who really matters is being put to the bottom of the pile – the reader, the listener, the viewer. I know, it's obvious when we think about it. But that's half the problem: we're so busy being clever that we don't think about what we're really trying to say and who we're saying it to. When we do, it makes the job so much simpler.

It's much easier to prepare the message when the foundation stones are laid. No good building the house on shaky ruins!

Given that words have so meaning different meanings and connotations, we need to look at the direction in which our message is going. Is the overall picture positive or negative? It may well be that you have got both some good news and bad news to relay.

Imagine your presentation is a bit like a weather forecast, starting off cloudy with some showers but getting sunny later on. In other words, unless it's a wedding speech, when hopefully the invited speakers are not going to be letting the bride and groom down, it's likely that you will have a general theme with lots of light and shade being threaded through.

If you do have some bad news to give out, you can soften the blow by saying it in a more positive or empathetic way. It's important that you choose your words carefully throughout so that you are saying exactly what you intend to say in a clear, understandable way and it's not going to offend anybody!

When you're writing your script, write it conversationally. Abbreviate your words and only use language you would use when you're talking to somebody else. The trap the majority of novice speakers fall into is to try to read out the written word. I don't deny this can be an intellectual challenge to anyone brought up on the traditional three Rs and who believes in writing impeccable English. Absolutely nothing wrong with that – except that reading aloud that kind of writing sounds dreadful and does nothing for your delivery! When it comes to speech making, think conversationally and write conversationally.

Keep it Simple is the key. Subclauses and rambling sentences are out of the question. It's fine to write short sentences and, dare I say it, even start them with And and But. It's almost as if writing like this is the magic formula to a good speech or presentation.

Remember we've got to make it easy on the listeners' ears. If you say something that sounds strange, they'll wonder what you meant or ponder over how odd it sounded. Keep them present and hooked in. Don't use gobbledegook or jargon.

We talked earlier about finding a framework for your speech and targeting a specific audience, and you can now also consider the type of person you are talking to and how you might address them.

- If they are someone who responds in a logical way they are going to be thinking and reflecting on what you have to say. Their kind of language will include words like deciding, considering and thinking, explaining.
- If a person responds in a kinaesthetic way, in other words to feelings and sensations, they will relate to words which are about the senses and feelings – about being comfortable and uncomfortable.
- What about the visual person, who understands and relates to things in pictures. You give them information they can visually respond to. If you asked them to see or picture something they would be exactly on your wavelength.
- Then there's the auditory person who relates by sound. You might use words like 'hear' or 'sound'. Are you hearing me? Can you hear what I'm saying?

Exercise

Before you start attempting to speak all four languages at once, try to discover what language you use. Tuning into what you say to yourself and others is a very useful exercise anyway, because you can also watch out for any sabotaging negative messages that you may either be giving yourself or sending out to others.

Once you've mastered your self-monitoring then you can begin to listen out for how others speak and the kind of code they use! It can be very helpful to understand what kind of person you are dealing with.

If you think they filter information through in a logical way then you're more likely to get them to understand you if you talk to them in an analytical way. If they are emotionally wired up, then talk to them on a feeling level. Kinaesthetic people will tend to go inside for their answers rather than looking on the outside. They will use vocabulary like hold, connect, strike, touch, frustrated, feel, fed up, connect.

The person who responds in an auditory way will hear what you have to say more easily if you talk to them on that level. Use words like ring, beat, tune, attune, dialogue, sound, listen, tell, loud, soft, voice.

The conceptual person who responds logically will be able to relate to language like motivate, comprehend, process, discernment and choice.

This is perhaps a good moment to briefly revisit the assertive versus the passive and aggressive modes of communication that we talked about in the chapter on Voice.

However strongly you may feel about something, your audience may not agree with you. Do not use language that makes you right and them wrong. It's imperative that you use words and phrases that draw your audience in and doesn't alienate.

Make sure that when you're talking about opinions you let the person on the receiving end know where it's coming from. If it's your point of view, own it! You might use phrases like:

- Well, in my opinion ...
- In my experience ...
- I have found ...

If it's a company policy (that perhaps you don't agree with) then without getting yourself into a politically difficult situation you can say:

- The company believes ...
- Our policy is ...
- Our mission statement says ...
- Our collective goal ...

There is nothing worse than having someone tell us what we're thinking or feeling. So avoid the temptation to say 'you' when you mean 'I', or to use 'we', on the assumption that your audience agrees with you. To be included in somebody else's belief system without being invited to give our own view or opinion is thoroughly alienating. Nothing can disconnect your audience more quickly than feeling livid about something you've said that is the polar opposite of their belief system. They are likely to think you are arrogant for assuming you know how they feel or think. You haven't had the courtesy to check out what they may believe and it's quite obvious that you think your opinions are the only ones that count!

Get them hooked in

One of the difficulties many speakers have is that, because they know their own subject-matter like the back of their hand, they find it hard to believe that it's still going to interest an audience when they're delivering the same type of information for the thousandth time.

If you've had the experience of passing on some new information to a group of people, or even an individual, it's certainly rewarding when you see their faces light up and the fact or experience you've just related to them make sense. Better than that when the piece of information you give them provides them with a life-changing moment.

It's important to remember, in a situation like that, that you have the expertise in a subject-matter which you are passing on to them. OK, so they may have heard it before but even so it will still serve as a good reminder.

By thinking of anecdotes and perhaps a couple of the more interesting statistics you can get your hands on you are going to wow your audience. We will look in more detail at hooking them in and keeping them hooked in the section on Presentation. But come up with a dynamic intro and a hard hitting conclusion and the rest of your speech will write itself.

Avoid jargon

What might seem familiar to you might be quite alien to someone else. I remember that, when I first moved into business circles, one of the words that baffled me was 'outsourcing.' I just couldn't grasp it as a word that people would actually use. Of course to anybody in the business world it makes complete sense and they would probably be surprised that it could possibly be misunderstood. It's one neat word that sums up giving work to outside companies. But certainly if you talked to the average person in the street they wouldn't know what you were talking about. So if there's the slightest risk that someone in your audience might be wondering what you're talking about, use the word, but briefly explain its meaning.

Worse still are codes and acronyms or abbreviations that are only familiar to those in the know! It can totally exclude your audience if you start talking about something that makes them feel left out. Not knowing what someone's talking about can lead to the person on the receiving end feeling ignorant and rather foolish and then they'll be so busy giving themselves a hard time in their heads they'll completely lose track of what you're saying!

One of the key foundation stones to build on when you're preparing your speech is to ensure that your audience can identify with at least some of the content.

By all means be controversial but you don't want to alienate the very people you're trying to get on your side. For example if you're hoping for a vote at the end, you have to imagine you're selling them a product you truly believe in.

If you are not convinced they are certainly not going to be.

Equally you have to be balanced and show you've done your research. It's no good doing the hard sell in a product, a belief or a new strategy unless you have looked at the potential pitfalls as well as the advantages. Seeing the overall picture will give you the credibility and recognition you deserve.

If you want to wow your audience, you have to come up with either a good story, some stunning facts or a great joke. All a bit risky because some of these things can go badly wrong. Start off with a bad joke and you can be in real trouble. You never know in these politically correct days who you might offend.

Going back to the idea of a framework, you need to know who you are addressing and what your message is. What are they going to go away with? Wouldn't it be great if hours, days, months down the line you were still being quoted. Well, give them something to quote!

It's about starting off powerfully and ensuring that somehow you can keep their attention.

Repetition is useful. If you have a theme you are working with, it's fine to go back and remind your audience what the focus and intention of your speech or talk is. Keep your language simple. Remember, less is more. If you use statistics then round them off. Don't start using decimal points; they won't be easily understood by your audience.

Even if you have something negative to say, try to phrase it in a positive way! Give a silver lining wherever you can. If you want to motivate and inspire you need to have that positive outlook. A seemingly negative experience can be a beneficial learning experience and the way in which you phrase something can make all the difference as to whether your audience can hear what you're saying and take it on board. You need to be encouraging and persuade your audience to stay with you and take away a message that's going to make a difference to their lives and to their work. Even if that's just a really good joke.

Some of the best talks I have ever been too are the ones where the speaker's related a hard luck story that has led them to great success. I love to hear how individuals have overcome adversity and used their negative experiences to change their life for the better.

One such talk that comes to mind was a man in the banking world who'd been invited to talk to small businesses in my local area. I went along to please my bank manager and prepared myself for cold soggy vol-au-vents and an evening of stultifying boredom. I was in fact bowled over by the speaker, who was a real character and used humour throughout his presentation. He told this tale of woe, with an impoverished upbringing and early years of poverty in his marriage. He recounted how he used to walk his dog each evening round the smart neighbourhood a few streets away from where he lived and gaze at the smart cars parked in the driveway. The more he did that evening walk, the more determined he became that he too would live in that street with a Rolls Royce parked outside. His vision and determination paid off. Some years later he was a millionaire and living in his dream house.

His story was inspirational not just in its content but in the way he told it. We heard about the bad times but also how they had served as a launch pad into his own successful career. And now here he was passing on his expertise and inspiration to all of us. OK, so that's more about content, but his language was upbeat and confidence-boosting. He certainly made me feel I could go out there and be my best.

Think about how you can make your speech or presentation more upbeat and inspiring. Instead of using words like 'can't,' 'won't,' 'impossible,' try phrases like 'here's how this can work for you', or 'try this one…'

Finally, your talk or speech is transient. They only have that one chance to hear what you're saying. Keep it simple. That makes for powerful, dynamic content.

4. COMMUNICATION
It's a Two-way Process

'Communication is the secret of success – pass it on.'

Communication is the most essential form of dialogue between human beings. It doesn't even have to be vocal; it's how we pass information from one person to another, whether through words, signs, pictures or gestures.

Communication in essence sends a message from one person to another. But unfortunately it's not always as simple as that. Our interpretative processes and feelings, cultural differences and language difficulties, can all get in the way. It's a reciprocal process; communicating isn't as simple as sending one message from A to B – there are a few bends in the road! Remember, what you intend and what is actually received can be quite different. So successful communication is about planning your message, keeping it simple, and delivering it with focus and intention.

Gary Owston is a professional voice coach and this is how he sees clear communication.

'Clear communication … that's what we want. And in normal everyday situations that is what we achieve. It's easy. We don't have to analyse or think too much about how we do it.

When we communicate we constantly assess: who we are, what we are saying, to whom we are speaking, our relationship with them, what we want, how we get it, the chemistry of the dialogue, the emotional impetus, the distance the voice has to travel and the environment in which it is operating. This is a process that has evolved over years of practice, from our first scream for food. During that time the body has established a routine, a habit. And our bodies are very happy to stay in a routine, it's safe, comfortable, stable.

However, we sometimes ask the body to change and that's when things can, and often do, go wrong.

If we are not sure who (or why) we are, we struggle to find the words to make sense of the self and the world. When we are not sure what we are saying the listener strains to make contact with the speaker and the result is confusion. When the relationship is unsure or strained, all sorts of life-games come into play and complete honesty is curtailed.

If there is no clear objective behind communication, the energy is lessened and the message will not travel. How we achieve the objective is to do with what we say, but it is also the tone or tenor of voice used, e.g. we can work the situation through empathy, sarcasm, silly-sweetness, belligerence, etc.; without an attitude behind words, speech can become flat, boring, dull.

The chemistry of communication is based on a process of continual analysis; in other words, we continually monitor what effect we are having and whether or not we have to change any aspects to achieve our objectives. This will determine the dynamic of the delivery. If we cannot see and therefore judge how far the voice has to travel we simply don't project to the listener. The environment, the physical setting where the communication takes place, may be pitch black, unbearably light, inside or outside, across heavy traffic or on the phone; wherever it is we make adjustments to carry the message clearly to the receiver.

We sometimes ask the voice to operate in unnatural or unfamiliar situations, e.g. the actor who has to speak, sing, recite other peoples' words; the orator who has the pressure of communicating their point of view to a large number of people; the speechmaker at a christening, wedding or funeral; the salesperson with their folio of rhetorical sound-bites; the presenter at a conference or seminar.

What happens then? The body, being a natural protector, will send out alarm signals. The breath supply will be taxed to give more energy; the speaker may think that the voice is located solely in the neck/mouth areas and start to push and unnaturally force the sound; tensions may arise in any part of the body to compensate for the alien situation; physical alignment will be altered; emotions and fear may cause the voice to stop working altogether. The body is protecting itself, saying that this is not normal, not routine, 'Stop!' Over a period of time, of course, the body will find ways of coping, it survives, but there is a real risk that coping will be based on an unnatural physical process.

But we want to carry on. So we have to analyse what is happening and learn how we can correct the metabolism so that the voice operates safely.

That is where voice teachers come in. A good voice teacher will first of all identify the problem and then find a series of exercises that will coax the body into believing that these experiences are just new and not dangerous. Once the voice feels safe the process will concentrate on the communication of the text.

What is a 'good voice'? One that works optimally and supports whatever is to be spoken; one that is clear so that the message gets through first time; one that prioritises what is to be said rather than how. One that the listener does not notice.

To develop a good voice, you need:

- good alignment
- a fair degree of fitness and flexibility
- diaphragmatic breathing rather than clavicular, (i.e. employing the stomach muscles rather than the shoulders)
- optimal functioning of the larynx (the larynx, sometimes called "the voice box", is a tubular structure in the neck where sound begins); the sound needs to radiate through the whole body, not just the neck and mouth
- good enunciation so that words are clearly defined
- a sense of dynamics so that the text is not flat, monotonic, boring
- and a good balance of muscular work so that things operate with ease, not lax or tense.

The communication of the text has to be a part of you. The actor who meticulously creates a character, almost to the point of metamorphosis, will have more basis for speaking a kind of 'truth' than one who simply speaks the lines and misses the furniture. The orator who seems to be speaking extempore will be more effective than one who keeps referring to, or, worse, reading from, notes. The speech-maker at a social gathering should think carefully about what they want to say as well as what they think the audience wants to hear. The salesperson's blurb, whether it be door-to-door, at a market place or in a specific meeting, will be more effective if he considers the rapport to be established (i.e. the personal connection) first, and then gets on to how much information has to be delivered, over what period of time, how the listener will digest the information and when to mention money!

One should remember that listening to someone speak from the heart, with honesty, desire, investment, clarity, and preferably, eye contact, is the most effective way of delivering a message.'

But what happens when, for whatever reason, you can't communicate or express yourself well verbally?

Emma is in her twenties and works with children suffering from autism.

'When considering fundamental human dignities and basic human rights, the right to communicate must be near the top of that list. The ability to make one's needs and feelings known and, perhaps most importantly of all, the right to say 'no' cannot be emphasised enough as an integral part of the route to independence and the foundation of social relationships.

In my own profession I experience first-hand the dire consequences lack of communication can bring. Perhaps the most obvious effect this has upon the individuals I work with is a build-up of frustration which leads to alarming negative behaviours such as self-harm.

I cannot adequately convey the experience of witnessing a toddler head banging a wall through sheer frustration at not being understood. But perhaps more subtly at first, this lack of 'voice' also impacts heavily upon the individual's independence; how can they ask for help, form social relationships, friendships when they are the 'kid that doesn't talk'? How can they realise their potential when this lack of communication is invariably mistaken for a lack of intelligence?

The ability to be understood is what sets humans apart from the rest of the animal kingdom and this lack of effective communication is what sets an individual apart from the rest of society.'

Being heard, being listened to in the truest sense of the word is vital to our well-being and connected at a fundamental level to how we see ourselves.

COMMUNICATION IN THE WORKPLACE

We spend 70 per cent of our waking time communicating. The bad news is that, according to researchers, 90 per cent of the problems in the workplace are blamed by employees on poor communication. What is poor communication? It's when the message isn't received in the way it was intended. But bettering our communication skills is down to practice. It's a learning curve and an experiential one at that.

Lizzie is a bank manager who has been practising the art of clear communication with her staff.

'Communication is vital to ensure my team feel valued, informed and motivated. I have, in the past, found it difficult to speak regularly with all of my team of twenty-eight people, and communication and coaching was something I was going to do if I could find the time.

I knew that I could get the best out of my team by talking with them on a daily basis. The days that I made that effort were the best days in terms of business, personal development, motivation and fun. A top-performing football manager wouldn't expect his team to run onto the pitch without setting out the strategy for the match. Who does what and when. So I realised that it was imperative that I run team talks at the start of each day.

These take the form of a short, snappy summary of the previous day, including recognising performance, sharing best practice and ideas. I then cover the events of the day ahead, concentrating on the business objectives. Each member of staff is encouraged to 'buy-in' to these objectives by bidding for their own daily target. These targets are put on a white board which is updated throughout the day. The meeting is then summarised and all the team go to their jobs knowing clearly what direction and objectives they will be aiming for. The board is updated at half-time (lunch breaks) by the team players and where coaching is needed this is booked in for after lunch to help support them in reaching their goals by the end of the day. Of course where half-time targets are exceeded, people are praised and encouraged to share their best practices with the rest of the team.

During the afternoon, I build an hour or two into my day to observe and coach my staff by using the GROW coaching model. GROW stands for Goal, Reality, Options and Will. Reality is where you are at the moment. Goal stands for where you want to be. Options is what you can do about it and Will is how determined you are to get there. This model helps people to identify their weak areas and come up with their own solution to improve and work differently to achieve their goals. I document these sessions and set a time to revisit the plan, which is agreed with the team member.

At the end of the day we all get together again more informally for about five minutes to collect the final scores and to praise individuals for their contributions. We also discuss top sales tips and what worked and what didn't. This meeting has the effect of closing the day and clearing minds ready to start again the following day.

Since I have shifted to communicating in this way, I have achieved the business goals I set out to achieve and have a challenged, motivated, skilled and happy team.

Having understood why communication is so vital, and the importance of team talks, half-time scores, coaching and end-of-day summaries, I needed to be much tougher with myself to ensure that these were happening without fail.

I drew myself up a daily planner and specific time slots to deal with administration, business development, phone messages, returning letters and visiting my other two sites. I avoid straying from the plan and try to keep as near as possible to the time scales. This has had a positive effect on my day-to-day running at the branch. I have learned to say no to interruptions and find that I achieve a great deal more in terms of communicating with and developing my team, a part of my role which I find enjoyable and rewarding.

I have found that, by using a planner, I can be sure the tasks will be done and prioritised. A few months ago I was juggling four or five tasks at once and achieving very little, especially in terms of coaching and developing my team.

I have built trust and respect by being challenging, fair and honest. I believe that you should treat others the way you would like to be treated yourself. I have followed this for years and it works with every individual and every situation even when there is confrontation or conflict.

To give developmental feedback you should reflect back what happened, how it made you feel, or the impact it had, and provide a suggestion on how to change or improve the situation. For example, "Michelle, when you said ... it made me feel ... which had the effect of ... perhaps you could try ...". By giving feedback in this way, you are letting people know how you are feeling, which can make it very personal to both of you.

You can also gain respect and trust by taking the time out to explain how their actions can impact business decisions. For example, I had a situation where a team member had requested their birthday as leave. However it was difficult to authorise as I had the maximum number of staff on their holidays already. I sat down with the staff member and explained the difficulties and the impact it would have on the rest of the team and the business. I then asked her what plans she had for the day. She replied she was going out for the evening and wanted to get ready. So we reached a compromise and agreed that she leave at 3pm to prepare for her celebrations.

The outcome was she was delighted that she could go early and I was pleased it had a minimal effect on the business whilst still earning me respect for reaching a compromise. The longer term result was also positive as this team member will now always be flexible with her working hours wherever possible. This in turn has had a good effect on the rest of the team who have become more flexible as well!

Successful communication is about getting a good end result. You can't be prescriptive about the route you take but what you're aiming for is getting your message heard and understood.'

Have the courage to go for it. It is a learning curve and you will get better at communicating the more you work at it.

Remember what you give out, you get back. Invest in improving your communication skills and it will transform you and your life!

5. PRESENTATION SKILLS
How to Put on a Great Show

You never get a second chance to make a first impression.

How we dress, act and speak all counts towards that first impression. It goes without saying that, however liberal-minded we like to think we are, we probably judge or jump to conclusions about a person within seconds of meeting them.

DRESS

Dress is a social statement. It gives lots of signals about who we are, our attitudes and the messages we want to give other people. We might have an extensive or diverse wardrobe; certain clothes for certain occasions; and that's fine. It's just important to ensure we choose our outfits carefully when it comes to making our presentation.

Again, we have to consider the occasion and our audience. In the section on Media skills we will cover specific dress codes and what not to wear when faced with the television cameras, but for this chapter we're looking at the generalities of dress.

At the risk of sounding sexist, it seems to me it's probably an easier and more limited choice for men! Suits, shirts, ties, blazers ... but for the woman, is it the little black suit, the skirt and shirt, the smart trousers and top or the floaty chiffon look?

Apart from the obvious requirements, I believe it's really important to feel comfortable about what you're wearing. That's more likely to happen if you turn up wearing something similar to your audience. There's nothing worse than arriving to discover you're in black tie and your audience look like they've just arrived from the beach. You will think of nothing but how much you stand out and how inappropriately you have dressed for the occasion and that may sabotage your imminent speech or address.

A man recently told me he had a special suit he wore to high-profile occasions because he knew he felt confident wearing it. In many ways it's not just about what other people will think of us, but perhaps even more importantly what we think about ourselves. Feeling good on the inside is at least half the battle for a good performance.

It's back to preparation. Never worry about asking too many questions beforehand, because it'll be too late by the time you're there. Questions to ask yourself – is it daytime or evening? What about the temperature, climate, culture? If it's an evening do just after work hours then check out what other people are wearing.

I had a near-miss experience when I'd arranged to go to a very smart hotel for a meal with an exclusive dining club. Frankly, I didn't really know what to wear because it began at seven in the evening and I wasn't sure if everyone else would be going straight from work in their suits. I decided to compromise and donned the semi-smart but casual look. A friend and colleague of mine turned up to collect me looking stunning in a calf-length silk jacket and wonderful, glamorous jewellery.

With five minutes to spare I rushed upstairs to change! Only problem was I still didn't know what to change into and, even worse, I'd put on a few pounds and couldn't fit into the obvious choices. Half an hour later, with about ten outfits scattered around the bedroom floor, I didn't know whether to laugh or cry. My friend, obviously feeling quite desperate for me, asked if I'd actually paid for my ticket – the inference being that perhaps I should give it a miss. I had paid for my ticket and I knew I couldn't bottle it. Eventually I found something that I felt reasonably comfortable in and turned up trying to look cool rather than frantic.

I couldn't help but be amused when someone I had done some coaching work with came up to me and said had anyone else ever told me I looked like a 1950s movie star?!! They hadn't, and I don't, but I felt flattered if not fraudulent knowing the shambles that had gone on earlier! Nevertheless it made me realise that, however flatteringly others see us, if we don't feel comfortable in our skin then it gets in the way. It takes up an awful lot of head space!

If in doubt, dress in a neutral way. For example, if you are chairing a debate on a controversial subject, then you won't want to wear clothes that will make one half of your audience believe you are on their side and the other half against them. It sounds so obvious but I have come across many situations where the first thing I've noticed is somebody's outfit. They may be deliberately trying to make a statement, but equally I may have already bracketed them into some category which may not even be the right one to put them in.

So the Number One Rule about clothing is to find out what type of event it is and ask the organisers what people are expected to wear. If you get an open-ended answer, then just ensure you go in something you feel good in. It's how confident and motivated you are on the inside that really counts.

These days it seems an informal approach to dress is much more acceptable – but not in every situation. If you turn up in an open-necked shirt, casual trousers and no tie and discover everyone else in formal dress that will make for a very uncomfortable experience for you.

In his book *Peoplewatching*, Desmond Morris makes the interesting point that clothing acts as a signal. He suggests that the skirt length of the modern western world acts as an economic barometer – as hemlines rise and fall, so does the financial climate of the country!

BODY LANGUAGE

This leads on to the question of body language. There isn't a sign or gesture we make which doesn't contain a subconscious message of some kind. A basic understanding of body language is immensely helpful when it comes to giving out positive signs to others. Understanding our gestures and those of others is important because it can help us to feel more empowered in situations. For example, if someone is giving us a hard time but we can see by their body language that they are uncomfortable or insecure about what they're saying, then it helps us gauge a more appropriate response.

We must remember that non-verbal skills are still communication skills. How much can we tell from someone's facial expressions or body gestures? Research has shown that what we say and how we say it accounts for less than than 35 per cent of the message and that 65 per cent of our communication is non-verbal.

We have already touched on the importance of intuition in other sections of the book; having a sixth sense about someone or just 'knowing' something is a very powerful non-verbal clue. I like the idea that our intuition is our inner alarm system. It's usually not what someone says but something about the way they say it that can give us a much greater understanding about what's really going on.

It's said that women are generally more in touch with their intuition then men. They are more likely to have a hunch or sixth sense about something. But as society as whole takes more interest in looking at inner self-development, it seems that men too are being encouraged to work with their intuition.

The fact is that how someone looks and their body language are two factors that strike us immediately when we meet someone. Clothes, hair and the expression on someone's face give us clues. We may well form opinions about them on these facts alone. Sometimes that isn't fair and we come to see there's much more to someone than we assumed when we first met them. Or later on we can see we put them in the wrong box!

Experts say that it is difficult for us to control our body language because it tends to be illustrating what's going on inside – our emotional reactions. And body language can be a big clue as to our personality.

Some body movements can be conscious, others unconscious. It's not so much a matter of looking at somebody and working through their body language signals top to bottom but, rather, getting a general sense of who they are and what's really going on. Non-verbal communication is like having a second set of signposts and we should learn to read them!

But what we might interpret in one culture or society could mean something completely different in another. Also one isolated gesture is not a great way to interpret the full meaning of what someone is saying. You have to take into account all the body gestures you observe.

As Allan Pease says in his book on *Body Language: How to Read Others' Attitudes by their Gestures*, a gesture cluster – a set of signals – is like a full sentence. You should also consider whether what the person is saying matches their body language, and take into account the context. But experts in this field claim it's simply not possible to lie with your body language. You might get away with it as far as verbal communication is concerned but your body language will be the give-away!

Eyes

One of the first points of contact is the eyes. If our eyes are the windows of our soul, then looking into someone's eyes can reveal their inner truth. Research has shown that when our pupils dilate or contract, it is indicative of mood; dilated pupils indicate excitement, while contracted pupils are a sign of anger or negative feelings. Often when we see pictures of criminals or serial killers they have that cold, distant look in their eyes.

How we use our eyes is another factor. How long we gaze at someone or can focus our attention on their eyes can reveal a great deal about how we are feeling. When someone can't look us in the eyes, what does that say? Conversely, when a person is comfortable with looking at someone directly, this is usually a positive sign. It is helpful to imagine that a person's face contains a triangle formed of the mouth and the two eyes, and to look at that area, shifting your gaze between their eyes and lips. It means you are not going to leave them feeling disconcerted by staring intently into their eyes.

Because eye contact is so important, we should not put it to the bottom of our list when it comes to presentation skills. If we are faced with a large audience, that ability to keep eye contact is obviously more challenging. But it is also essential. If you can connect with everyone in that audience at some point it is a big bonus. They will automatically feel you are interested in getting your message across to them and you are developing the skill of telling your story to one person.

I know that when I have attended conferences or lectures, the ones I have gained more knowledge from are those given by a speaker or lecturer who engages me, rather than concentrating their focus on just one person in the room. That in itself is exclusive and excluding; it may make the person who's been targeted feel distinctly uncomfortable and everyone else in the room will feel left out.

A technique that I have personally tried to develop over the years – and I have to say that though it can feel somewhat unnatural it does work – is to be aware and focused enough to remember to look round the room, and I mean right round the room, because it's easy to leave out the people on the far left or far right. Even if you don't literally connect with their eyes it's a gesture that will help to get them hooked in and listening to you.

Expression

What about our expression? Well, a bit like clothes, we have to make sure we match our message. If you are about to deliver a serious or sombre message, it won't set the scene well if you grin inanely before you start. But generally speaking, a sincere smile will serve you well and put your audience at ease.

57

Equally, it's OK to smile and then pause before you launch into what you're about to say. In fact the Pause, as we discovered in the chapter on Voice, can often say more than any words. It gives breathing space for you as the speaker and for your audience.

Non-verbal communication

Experts on body language have identified various techniques to help us determine what non-verbal communication means. One of them is a memory technique or mnemonic device, SO CLEAR.

S is for sitting and standing and the way in which you make the most of your space. If you avoid sitting directly opposite someone this sends a message of openness and not one of confrontation. It is important not to crowd in on someone or even stand too close to the front row of your audience. Otherwise it's like being at the front of the cinema, when you're looking up at the big screen and totally enveloped by the sound and pictures. It can be too much.

Here are some guidelines for avoiding invading someone's personal space:

- Intimate zone: if you're with your partner or family, you will stand near enough to be able to touch them. That's between 15 and 50cm.
- Personal zone: if you're with friends or close colleagues, then you can stand between 50cm and 1.2m.
- Social zone: if it's an acquaintance, then between 1.2 and 3.5m
- Public zone: this is people you don't know; with a large group of people gauge your distance at over 3.5 metres.

To keep it simple, think of the expression an arm's length. This is a good rule of thumb when it comes to social and business situations.

O is for openness. If you hunch yourself up and cross your legs and arms, you are literally closing up and that kind of body position gives off hostile signals. Equally, holding any of your features tightly, like pursing your lips or clenching your fists, can give the impression of not wanting to hear what the other person has got to say. If you make open body gestures and look like you are interested in what the other person has to say, it creates a spirit of openness and receptiveness.

C is for centring your attention on the person you are talking to. Focus is such a key word for any kind of communication. If you are focused, you are present and able to speak and listen far more clearly. Giving someone your undivided attention is the highest compliment you can pay them. It makes them feel heard and valued. And they are far more likely to hear what you've got to say when they feel you are interested in them.

L is for leaning. Leaning forward when you're listening to someone is signalling interest in what they are saying and it's another way of asking them to tell you more. It's a good technique as long as you don't move uncomfortably into their body space! Leaning back slightly can take the pressure off someone. But if you lean too far back you can look like you're so laid back you're falling over.

E is for eye contact. As I said earlier, the eye contact is critical. You can tell so much from someone just by eye contact alone. It is a sign of interest. If you don't look at someone properly it can give a signal of being uninterested.

A is for being at ease. How at ease do you feel when you communicate? If you seem nervous, distracted or over-excited this can be very off-putting. But if you seem at ease with yourself and with the other person it makes for great communication. That kind of body language enables both parties to really hear each other and get their message across.

How you sit or stand is important. Standing tall or sitting up straight is a physical and mental reminder to keep focused and uncluttered!

R is for reflecting and responding. Reflective listening responses are a sign we are being attentive to what the other person has said to us. Repeating back, albeit in a different way, shows we have understood what they have said. It's also a good way of avoiding misunderstandings.

READING BODY LANGUAGE

As we've discovered, body language can sometimes say far more than we can articulate in words. It gives off numerous positive and negative signals. It is important to be able to read these non-verbal gestures because it can help with how we present ourselves and how we respond to a person.

Barriers

Arm-crossing can be a signal that a person feels under threat and is trying to protect themselves. Interestingly not only does arm-crossing worry the speaker but research has shown that, when people make a defensive gesture like this, they cannot retain as much of the information being given to them as the person who keeps their arms open.

Folding both arms across the chest may be a sign of insecurity or suggest that someone feels threatened.

If someone clenches their hands it suggests they're frustrated. You can tell the level of frustration by how high their hands are.

Crossed leg gestures are a negative sign. Even though culturally many of us might cross our legs, that kind of gesture can be seen as a barrier. Apparently, if you cross your arms and your legs you have effectively signalled that you have stopped taking part in whatever's going on.

Guarded behaviour

If a person covers their mouth with their hand and their thumb is up against the cheek, it may be a sign they are trying to suppress deceit. If they cover their mouth while you are speaking, it can be a sign they think you are not being truthful.

Rubbing your eyes or ears can be linked to the 'see no evil, hear no evil' mantra; a sign that someone is trying to block out deceit in some way, or to not hear the words that are being spoken. The phrase 'lying through your teeth' indicates that a person puts on a false smile by clenching their teeth; and rubbing their eye at the same time would be a gesture cluster.

One particularly interesting piece of research has shown that when someone tells a lie it causes a tingling feeling on the face or neck which they need to scratch.

Decision-making gestures

If you are presenting a concept or idea to an audience, you are likely to find that the majority of people will start to use evaluation gestures, demonstrating that they are thinking about what you are saying. They may stroke their chin as they form an opinion or make a decision about whatever it is you've said. If someone has their hand on their cheek it can be a sign of interest. On the other hand, if they use their hand to prop themselves up, you could interpret that to mean they are bored by what you're saying.

On a personal and cautionary note, I have to say that on the occasions I have allowed myself to be distracted by the body language of a member of the audience, I have not always correctly interpreted their non-verbal movements. It can be very distracting to see someone looking bored or uninterested in what you have to say, and the danger is that you will disengage from what you're saying and start worrying about what they're thinking about you.

And sometimes I have got it completely wrong. The person I have assumed is disapproving of me in some way is likely to be the person who will come up afterwards and say how much they got from the presentation!

So my rule of thumb when it comes to presentation is that, while it can be useful to understand the body language of your audience, it is impossible to read each person's every gesture so don't allow yourself to get hooked into it at the expense of your presentation.

It is also important to take into account the fact that different cultures play a large part in body gestures and their interpretation. And while the crossed arms may signal defensiveness, somebody may just be cold, or they may have been taught when in school to fold their arms when they'd finished their work!

The essence of body language is whether the person seems open and receptive to what you have to say or whether they are closed down. Open body gestures versus closed body gestures. I also believe intuition comes into this. In my experience it is possible to feel or intuit what's going on.

Whenever I meet people who seem defensive through their body language or even their verbal communication, I assume they are trying to hide something. Arrogance and an apparently superior attitude can be an indicator of someone's nervousness or vulnerability. So don't be put off by what you see or feel; certainly don't take someone else's behaviour or attitude personally or think you have done something wrong, because it could well be a cover-up!

Positive body signals include:

- Relaxed and open body gestures
- Feet pointed towards you
- Good eye contact
- Thoughtful, acquiescent expression
- Body positioned in your direction
- Leaning forward
- Moving towards you

Negative body signals include:

- Fist clenching
- Poor eye contact
- Hand over mouth
- Leaning away from you
- Tapping foot or pencil
- Drumming fingers
- Tensed up
- Feet pointed away from you
- Wringing hands
- Putting hands through hair
- Stiff posture

Rapport

Some experts argue that mirroring someone else's body language can build rapport. I can't say I have tried this technique, as I tend to focus on what and how someone is talking to me, but it is suggested that we can build rapport through matching the people we are with. One thing's for sure, that when we've lived with someone for a long time we often pick up their verbal or facial expressions. In fact, I find it frustrating when I hear myself using language that my teenage kids use, or words that my partner uses that I normally wouldn't dream of saying!

But you can become aware of how someone else is talking and being. If they are speaking much more quietly than you are, it might be a good idea to soften your voice and match them. It will help the other person to feel more at ease and receptive to what you're saying.

Rapport means you are in harmony with someone else and is particularly important when it comes to delivering and receiving messages clearly.

PERFORMANCE CHECKLIST

You have done all your preparation, researched your audience, worked out your speech, got your cue cards and now you are faced with your actual performance.

Firstly, do you sit or stand at your lecture or presentation? I believe you should do what feels the most comfortable in the situation you are in. I find that unless I am placed at the front of a hall with a stand and lectern, I would rather match what the audience is doing. There are some arguments for standing because then you can project your voice better. But if you feel out of place during the whole of your speech then sit down, but sit up straight and get yourself into the focus position.

Now let's just go through that final checklist again:

1. It takes just fifteen seconds or so for us to decide what we think of someone. We take into account their clothes, hair and mannerisms. It's what known as the 'halo' effect.
2. But that initial perception can be bolstered or shattered by one very important factor – the voice! It's no good putting on the smart suit, spending hours on your hair (and make-up), and then not putting any thought into how you present yourself in terms of your mannerisms and your voice.
3. So when you walk into that room, remember your posture – look confident and as though you mean business. Good eye contact and a smile. If you're practising some of the new tips you've been reading about, take heart. Experts say it will take about a month to undo old habits and use your new skills. And apparently it takes about nine weeks to make that new skill a habit.
4. Open gestures can replace shut-down body language and research has shown that touching someone appropriately can increase the impact of your message by up to 300 per cent!

Sherrie is a successful radio and television presenter. Her roots are in Dominica, although she was brought up in Bristol. Her father instilled in her that education was the crucial path to success, and encouraged her to make the most of any opportunities in her life. As a child, Sherrie proved to be a good athlete rather than an academic.

'I was quite shy and never put my hand up in class. I certainly wasn't assertive and the thought of reading out loud in the classroom made me feel nauseous. Who would have thought that I would end up being the main anchor person fronting the local evening television news programmes and presenting documentaries. Not me for sure!

After twenty years in the business I am still glad to have the opportunity to look at my voice. I often have to give talks and presentations and it's important to be able to project your voice and speak clearly. It's something that people comment on and appreciate. I would just like to say that whatever our background, whoever we are in society, we are unique individuals with skills and a voice that can get us places.'

We may find ourselves having to give a presentation whatever our age or background. This schoolboy found his voice to come up with an unusual initiative that led the school to apply for a business grant which they successfully won – helped by a presentation given by the youngsters.

Merrick is twelve. Particularly keen on skateboarding. Not so keen on school. Now, thanks to putting his communication skills to good use, he enjoys both. When he started at his secondary school he made good progress. Bearing up on the academic front, he discovered his musical talents through forming a rock band with his friends. But he decided there was one more thing that would make school a bit more bearable – skateboarding facilities!

So entirely on his own initiative, he set about writing to the headmistress (and pasting in colourful pictures of ramps and skateboarders) and suggested they set up a skateboarding club. He had thought through the inevitable problems of funding and health and safety. He had approached a local skateboard shop owner and asked him to sponsor the club and asked for the teachers to oversee the club in the break times.

His headmistress was so pleased with his entrepreneurial skills that she agreed to the idea, subject to the parents' permission. A year on, not only is the skateboarding club a huge success and the envy of all the other kids in schools around the city, but it has formed the basis for the school's successful application for a £150,000 business and enterprise grant and specialist status.

As a result of this initiative, Merrick and two of his friends had to give a presentation to over fifty business people and local dignitaries. Scary for anybody but perhaps especially so for self-conscious adolescents. But Merrick actually enjoyed the experience because had had prepared for it: 'Once I knew what I was going to say and I had practised it, I found it really easy and enjoyed talking to the people. I think it was important to make eye contact and smile. We had to persuade the audience that skateboarding was a good leisure activity. I also found making them laugh helped a lot!'

6. MEDIA OPPORTUNITIES
Identify the Openings

These days it would be easy to think the media are almost exclusively the preserve of bloodthirsty paparazzi. True, it would be naïve to believe that the media exist for the sole purpose of promoting our personal or business aspirations. But I believe many people are put off even attempting some kind of relationship with the media because of the fear of repercussions.

Let me say from the outset nobody can make you say anything you don't want to. The trouble is that under the glare of the media spotlight it is all too easy to end up saying something you might regret later. In this chapter, and when we look at the subject of Interview skills in the next one, I will suggest simple and effective techniques to help you make the right contacts and prepare and deliver the best possible interview confidently and clearly!

Never feel you are at the mercy of the media. In fact, you should capitalise on every opportunity and create chances to get your name or your company in the headlines. Many people are frightened of the media and try to avoid it all costs rather than embracing the chance to get in print or on air.

How does the old maxim go? Any publicity is good publicity. In many ways that's true. Even if you are facing a controversial situation it is far better that you get your voice out there rather than someone else speculating on your behalf and probably getting their facts wrong.

You need to control the message, not the other way round.

If you are taking a proactive approach to the media there are lots of ingenious ways of getting yourself on air. It's worth considering that what you find interesting and what you enjoy reading about could be on your doorstep. There are many celebrities who've made their names through volumes of publicity. As we know, in today's world you can be famous for being famous.

I always encourage the police officers I train to see the media as part of their team. We are always happy to broadcast or print an interesting story. That in turn gives them a chance to run public appeals for information and often get their crimes solved more quickly.

If you are a company you could commission a survey, which will inevitably produce some interesting results or statistics that could well make a good story for the media. Think headlines.

If you discover that one of your employees is doing some amazing unique feat for charity, then get their story in the local paper and you might just get the company name in too. Whatever makes a good story in your local pub can also be newsworthy.

The health service can use the media not just to defend a shortage of beds or lack of cash but to promote new research findings or fundraising activities. The list is endless.

WHO ARE THE MEDIA?

But in order to make a considered decision on when a media opportunity can be seized, it's helpful to have a picture of who the media are, what their functions are and their different needs:

- Print: newspapers, magazines and the trade press.
- Radio: BBC and commercial network, independent, digital and community radio.
- Television: terrestrial network television, terrestrial regional television, satellite, cable and digital television.

In other words a plethora of channels which also equals a multitude of opportunities to get your message across. Although different programmes and news bulletins vie for viewers, cross-media ownership and close working relationships means much of the material is swapped and shared between individuals and companies which might be perceived by outsiders as rivals. But having said that, in my experience of working in newspapers, radio and television at regional and network level, any self-respecting journalist wants the story first!

Newspapers

There are national daily newspapers, Sundays and hundreds of local newspapers. It is vital to understand the differences in the beast you're dealing with. When I train groups to become more media-aware, I warn that the tabloids are a law unto themselves. Unlike broadsheets or trade magazines, they do not rely on good contacts they can go back to again and again. They are generally only interested in getting the scoop of the day at whatever price.

I am not trying to put you off doing interviews, far from it. But when you're dealing with a large national tabloid which makes its money from sensational headlines, you are less likely to be treated fairly.

The same cannot be said of local newspapers, which rely on good contacts for future stories as well as the ones they're writing at the time. In fact, your local weekly or daily newspaper can be a great way for you to promote yourself or your business. It's back to the basic rule of knowing your audience.

If you think about the reams of newsprint that are published every day of the year you can imagine why newspapers are keen to have your story. Don't assume they are doing you a favour, it's quite probable your new revolutionary product will be just the story they need to fill the gap on the inside pages. Even better if you give them the lead story that's going to make dynamic headlines and sell them extra copies.

Newspapers rely on sales because that is how they appeal to advertisers. Like all sections of the media, it is a cash-making business and that's its priority.

From your point of view it's important to think about the readership of the particular newspaper you are approaching. Just like researching your audience before you make your presentation, think about who you are trying to address before you send off your press release to a source.

Radio

Radio is informative, educational and entertaining. Radio is about establishing a close relationship with the listener. For some people, radio is their most constant companion. It goes without saying that successfully mastering radio is all about how you sound and how you use the airwaves. Radio embodies the concept of talking to one person. That listener is your audience and it's your job to hook them to what you're saying; to capture their imagination.

There are thousands of local radio stations throughout the country, as well as the major network and digital channels. The BBC has the World Service, local stations and BBC network radio. Not to mention the number of digital radio channels springing up. There are hundreds of commercial radio stations. As the media increases it also increases your choice. If you have a particular story or product you want to get on the airwaves, you can choose where to place it. Like any news organisations, radio newsrooms want the best story first. We will discuss how to get your message across with your interviews later, but understanding how radio works is important.

Again, research the audience. Your local BBC radio station is likely to have an older audience than, say, your local commercial radio station, which is probably more music-based. As a voice coach, it makes me shudder to hear some local radio stations playing music under their news bulletins! Spend some time listening to the station you hope to interest and then, when you approach them with your story, you will have an idea of how their interviews work in terms of their output.

Television

If radio is about sound, then television is about visuals. Always be aware of the picture and how you appear in front of camera. There is no doubt about it, you will be judged on appearance as well as content and sound.

In broadcasting generally, but specifically in television, it is the immediacy of the communication that matters. As an interviewee, you are both informing and performing at the same time. So it's important to be well briefed without sounding under pressure and relaxed without appearing uninterested. These things come with practice. You have to learn to be comfortable with your delivery, the sound of your own voice and how you appear.

Remember that television has a tendency to exaggerate any mannerisms you may have unconsciously picked up. While it is important to be animated, your mission is get your message across and understood. It's important to strike a balance so that you come over as real and interesting, rather than either tense and hyperactive or so laid back that you seem bored.

It's up to you find the balance that suits you but, broadly speaking, when you have a point to make, make it clearly and when someone else is talking, listen to what they're saying. There might well be a good opportunity for you to get another point in.

Television channels are increasing all the time. You have BBC and regional television stations, network BBC television and the network independent channels. There are dedicated news channels and satellite, cable and digital channels.

While this might all seem overwhelming if you are wondering where to pitch your message, remember that if you have a good story it's likely to be picked up by other media as well as your chosen one.

TIMESCALES

All these different newsgathering organisations work to different deadlines. It's vital that you find out what the deadline is as this will make it easier to gauge what your timing and deadlines need to be. Firstly, check with the newspaper, radio or television station when they need to have your information by, or when they need to do the interview and when it's going to be broadcast or published.

As a guide, newspapers are working to daily or weekly deadlines. A local newspaper reporter may still be there when you return their call a couple of days later, a national newspaper reporter most certainly will not. A press agency reporter will want to talk to you immediately and probably has a clear idea about what you should say!

Radio news bulletins are generally on the hour, with a half-hour programme around lunchtime and early evening. Radio has the fastest turnaround rate – that's the time it takes from the interview being recorded until it goes out on air. Digital editing means the piece can be topped and tailed in a few minutes. Radio newsrooms are comparatively undermanned so it's important to be as eloquent as possible. There isn't the luxury of someone spending ages editing your piece and making sure all your 'uhmms' and 'ahs' disappear.

Television journalists work to programme and bulletin deadlines. The main bulletins will be breakfast-time, lunchtime and evening; bulletins which run mid-morning or mid-afternoon usually have less priority. The peak-time television interviews will either be conducted in the studio or on location. By and large, studio time is set and the time you are offered is unlikely to be flexible. If you are being asked to give an interview on location, such as in your office, on site or at home, you may be able to negotiate the time to suit you rather than them.

USING THE MEDIA EFFECTIVELY

Once you have been approached for an interview, establish when and where the interview or quotes from it will appear. If you are asked by a freelance or agency journalist, find out if they have been commissioned for the piece they are doing or if it is a speculative venture on their part. If it's a broadcast journalist, establish whether the interview will be live, recorded 'as live', or recorded.

Establish who you are talking to, who they work for, and what context your information or interview will appear in.

Bear in mind that a journalist's first priority is to deliver a story of interest to their readers, listeners or viewers. You are effectively providing the content for a story that has to be to some degree informative and entertaining, and certainly readable, listenable or watchable. Journalists rarely work in isolation and even specialists and freelances will be working to an angle they hope will guarantee publication or broadcast of their material.

You are likely to be approached by journalists for one of two reasons. Either they're responding to a story generated by your own PR, or they are responding to a story generated from some other source, such as new government legislation, surveys or academic reports or, worse, scandal!

Be wary if you get a call asking for your views on a wide range of subjects. The journalist has probably been told to fish out a specific line to make their story stand up.

Promoting a good image of yourself and your company, and establishing a good rapport with your interviewer, means you must be up to date with developments in your particular field. Make sure you know your facts and quote them accurately. Dates and figures will enhance your credibility. Don't quote as reliable facts or statistics that you are unsure about.

If you misinform a journalist, he or she will be the one to take the rap, not you, but an offended journalist has a long memory so it may be some time before you are contacted again. It's galling when you see a rival quoted or interviewed time and again when they could have used you!

If possible, offer to come back with information you are unsure of. A busy journalist will welcome any offers of reducing their workload. If that fails, then be honest – say you don't know.

So to sum up:
· Find out why the journalist has contacted you
· Be sure of your facts and figures
· Offer to help
· If you know of a reliable alternative source for the information, hand it on.

MEDIA RELATIONS

Availability is the key. Journalists are used to getting a prompt reaction to their enquiries and they are not always sensitive to your own professional or personal demands. All they really care about is getting the story, and first if possible. If you want to improve your media profile, make sure you've got your mobile with you and be willing to hand out your home phone number, because journalists do not work nine to five. It's useful, if you've sent out a press release, to give a number where someone can contact you out of office hours or at weekends. An instant response to an enquiry will establish you as media friendly. Put your lunch before an interview request and you may unwittingly become classed as a reluctant interviewee.

Build up your media contacts. Try to establish a relationship with the people who contact you. That's not always as easy as it sounds if they are rushing between jobs or juggling other stories, but if you're friendly and competent then it all helps on the media relations front. Where it feels appropriate, ask them questions about themselves and their organisation and try to build a picture of who they are.

When you find yourself coming into regular contact with a journalist, news editor or programme producer, you might suggest lunch. Use these people as contact points in future dealings with that organisation.

Finally, remember that most people in the media are working under a great deal of stress. They prefer to save time where possible by using people they know and who have proved themselves as competent interviewees or reliable contacts.

It's always worth being polite and honest when dealing with the media. You never know when the local reporter who calls you at home in the middle of dinner may not end up as the editor of a nationally networked news programme.

- Be aware of the opportunity to put forward your views
- Make sure what you have to say is relevant
- When the phone doesn't ring – ring them!

PRESS MATERIAL

While your contract may not require that you take responsibility for preparing press material, it is always worth making the time to check and approve draft press releases and material that's going to be included in press packs.

It's also worth taking time to consider what makes an effective press release and the pitfalls that should be avoided. One basic rule is to make sure the reader has a grasp of the story in the first three lines of the press release. Can you create a banner headline or can you improve on the one offered? And make sure you include the answers to the five basic Ws.

'Your Favourite Sweet comes out of the Ice Age':
- What: a revolutionary method of making ice cream

- Why: it's reconstituted and needs no freezing
- Who: No Sweat Products Ltd
- Where: New Town
- When: in the shops this summer

A good press release will answer all these points clearly and concisely.

Next make sure the material is written in simple, concise and clear language. If not, then the story or message won't be understood. Don't use jargon ordinary people wouldn't understand. If you are introducing words specific to your business then make sure you explain what they mean. Once you have read through the material, use these very basic checks, which will apply to most releases:

- What is the message?
- How have I communicated the message - is it new, authoritative, funny?
- What do I want the audience to remember?
- How do I make sure it has an impact on the reader?

Jane Alexander is a journalist and author who has spent many years working for most of the national daily newspapers and numerous women's and men's magazines, and has written sixteen books. Her advice on press releases is as follows:

'A press release can make a journalist's day or be tossed in the bin before it's even out of the envelope. So what makes the difference? Before you send out that press release ask yourself these vital questions:

1. Is this a newsworthy story? In other words, why would a journalist be interested in this story? Read it out loud to yourself and be brutally honest: hot stuff or dull as dishwater? Is there a reason why a journalist should be interested in this story *now*? Does it link in with any particular season or follow up from anything in the recent news? Obviously the answer to this will vary according to your market, which brings me onto question two:

2. Am I sending it to the right person? Research your market *very* carefully and pick your journalist with care. If, for example, your company has just produced a wonderful new multi-vitamin, then that might be of interest to trade papers and possibly (if you can find something really wonderful about it) to general health pages. However it will be dumped by anyone else. If, on the other hand, you've got a product that's just been backed up by stunning new research (and is being used by a host of A-list celebrities), then feel free to send it to half of Fleet Street and beyond. Always check you've got the current person (people move very quickly) and spell their name correctly.

3. Have I summarised the story in the headline and first paragraph? Journalists are sent sackloads of press releases every day – they skim read and if you haven't caught them in the first few lines, you've lost them.

4. Are all the vital nitty-gritty questions answered in the rest of the release? If it's a book, what's the title, the author, the publisher, the price, the release date? If

it's a product, what's the name, the company, the price (and for how much product), stockists, mail order phone number/email etc. If there is a supporting website, always give the URL. There's nothing so irritating as having to phone or email because something simple like a price isn't there.

5. If need be, could a journalist write a short story on the basis of your release? This often happens, particularly in busy newspaper offices. Your release should have all the relevant information, plus a couple of juicy quotes (make sure it's clear who is giving the quote and their title, position, etc). If there is research data, always give the full references in a footnote.

6. Do you have any celebrities you can drop into the release? Obviously this one will depend on your market but (horrible but true) virtually all newspapers and consumer magazines will salivate over a hot celebrity case study or endorsement – providing your celebrity is sexy and not a faded has-been.

7. Give a personal name and contact number and email in case a journalist wants to follow up the story. Make sure someone will be available at all times – remember papers in particular work odd times when on deadline (for instance Sunday is a workday for most dailies). Ensure the person taking calls is knowledgeable or can swiftly get the necessary information.

8. Ideally have photographs available if relevant, preferably saved as jpg files which can be sent to journalists – but *only* if they request them. Never ever send huge attachments by email, or unsolicited graphics or photographs. These go straight into the trash bin and generate huge ill-will.

9. Have you checked your spelling and grammar? Journalists love words and hate to see them butchered. Abuse of apostrophes, for example, turns me very sour.

10. Have you sent your release in time for the publication's deadlines? Remember monthly magazines work generally four months ahead of time, so no point in sending out your Christmas press release to them in November. Check with each publication.

11. Oh, one last thing. If you're promoting a product, by all means include a sample (it makes sense). But please forget the gimmicky promotional gizmos – we're not fooled.'

7. INTERVIEW SKILLS
Learn to Give and Get the Best Results

Any interview is a potentially nerve-racking situation for any of us, whether we're going for a job or marketing our company. An interview is an opportunity for us to promote ourselves and our skills, but it can also present an occasion for us to let ourselves down by not being at our best. That, I can assure you, can only happen if you go unprepared. It has to be acknowledged that some people enjoy this type of situation more than others. But doing a good interview is a learned skill. It something we get better at the more we do!

In this chapter we will look at a variety of interview situations, all with the single common denominator of preparation and planning. As long as you have your mental filing cabinet up-to-date, you can't go far wrong. Be clear about who you are and what you have to offer, and you should succeed.

I have spent nearly thirty years as a reporter or interviewer in some media capacity or another. But I have to say it took being on the other side of the microphone and camera for me to realise just how daunting it can be to be the interviewee!

As it turned out, I had plenty of opportunities to hone those particular skills when I had my first book published. When asked if I would be happy to do a national and international publicity tour, I undertook the challenge with relish. It was only several radio and television interviews later that I realised just what I had taken on!

Now, I am not saying this to put you off; far from it, because I learned some great tips during that process. For example, I had prepared for all sorts of questions about the book, its content and the publishers. It hadn't really occurred to me that I had to research my own personal history. So when confronted with questions such as, 'What exactly inspired you to write this book …?' or 'When did you first know that …?', my mind went blank. I think I managed to blag my way through at the time. But it did make me realise that I needed to have a mental filing cabinet of anecdotes and stories to illustrate any questions I might be asked or points I wanted to make. While you may manage off the top of your head to dredge up something relevant, a bit of research and preparation means you can come up with the best possible story that perfectly illustrates what you're trying to say.

While I'm on the subject, another daunting few moments came when I was doing a live networked television programme with a well known TV presenter. Nerve-racking in itself, and made even worse by the fact that said presenter had food poisoning and had to keep rushing off-set to be sick, and then proceeded to ask me the same question seven times! I can tell you retrospectively that she actually provided me with a great chance to promote my book and fill the airwaves with anything I wanted to say! It is a total myth that the interviewer is always in charge of the interview. Simply not true.

Remember, nobody can make you say something you don't want to. They may try very hard and you may fall for one of the tricks but the reality is that you are, or should be, in control of what you are saying. When I was confronted with such a situation, I stayed calm and centred and at no point looked or sounded defensive. I answered some controversial questions by acknowledging what had been put to me, but then going off in the direction I wanted to, and apparently managed to appear a grounded, informed and interested interviewee. The publishers reckoned if I could get through that situation they would let me go to North America for a whirlwind tour of all the big cities.

I was delighted to be given such a chance and thoroughly enjoyed all the experiences I had in the States. But one telling moment came when I was wheeled into the NBC studio in New York for an interview on their networked breakfast television programme. The trouble with remote studios is they are remote. I found myself sitting in a solitary studio with a remote camera and a switched-off monitor, and relying only on the voice in my ear. When the moment came and they introduced me, luckily, because I have worked in television, I knew that at the mention of my name I was on camera. So I smiled my best smile and prepared for the interview itself.

Now we are going to look at the process of being interviewed and I will include tips on media interviews, but I thought that story was worth recounting. How often have we seen some unsuspecting person on the television, looking terrified, miserable, frightened or even bored when the camera switches to them and they don't even know they are on people's screens. It goes back to my favourite three words that count for everything:

• Preparation
• Focus
• Delivery

But let's go back to the basics of the interview process itself.

JOB INTERVIEWS

This is a situation that most of us are likely to face at some time or another in our lives. In general, in business terms, there are three types of job interview:

• There is the biographical interview, drawing on your CV; so run through it before the interview and be sure it is up-to-date.
• There is the competency-based interview, where you will face a structured series of questions about your skills and how far they match the job description.

- And there's the situation interview, where all applicants are asked the same set of questions; these types of interview tend to be for lower-grade positions.

In fact if you've got a job interview you're already more than halfway there. Bolster your confidence by reminding yourself that you have probably beaten hundreds of other applicants to get the interview and that your future employers are already impressed with your qualifications. And now you can have a chance to really shine and sell yourself. Preparation, needless to say, is the key to giving the best interview. You might think you know your CV, but if you haven't gone through it with a view to selling yourself in an interview situation then you could end up selling yourself short.

When I help people prepare for an interview, I often start the session by getting them to tell me their life story (well, the headlines anyway!). I would say that on every occasion I have heard the person deliver some fascinating information that would enhance their job interview. The trouble is, when we're talking about ourselves we don't necessarily think we are as interesting as other people. If, for example, you casually (but quite deliberately) mention that you spent your child-hood living in different countries and cultures, you are telling the interviewer or panel that you are adaptable and responsive to change. If you weave in some other colourful headlines, you are presenting an image of a person who is interest-ing, interested and has a great deal to offer.

Funny – appropriately funny – stories can show you have a good sense of humour, an essential ingredient for life in the workplace! Even if you don't recount every story or fact you planned for, at least you have them to hand if you need to pull them out of your mental filing cabinet.

A good starting point on the preparation front is to write down the headlines of your life. Also write a list of your positive qualities and your negative traits. Many people find it only too easy to come up with the negative traits and can barely muster up one positive thing to say about themselves. But remember an interview situation is a chance to sell you. And let's face it nobody wants someone who can only focus on the negative. There is an essential difference between being self-effacing and a complete no-hoper.

Ask yourself what you would expect from someone coming for the job interview you've applied for. What qualities are right for the job? Do you match them? What experiences can you talk about that show you're just the person they're looking for with the right combination of qualities?

You might well be asked to consider what might get in the way of your doing the best possible job. Again this is still an opportunity to promote yourself. You can mention your defects (or defect) but even better if you can describe a situation where that defect let you down but taught you something about yourself, and how you have now gained from that experience.

Think about your academic achievements and, just as importantly, your interests outside the workplace. For example, if you are an Outward Bound teacher at weekends, the interviewer will deduce that you are a good team leader with motivational skills, courageous and determined.

It's also very important to do your research about the company you are hoping to work for. It's almost inevitable they will ask you if you have any questions and it doesn't sound great if you don't. Knowing enough background about the firm or shop will enable you to ask interesting questions which will engage the people interviewing you. Do you know anyone who works there or has worked there? What are the employers like and what about pay and conditions? Remember, forewarned is forearmed.

Perhaps at this point I should also say it's a good idea, too, to research the area in which you are seeking the job. I guess we all have at least one disastrous interview to learn from. Mine was when I was attempting to leave the local evening newspaper in South Yorkshire where I had done my journalist's training for the past three years. I applied for a job on a commercial radio station in Glasgow and got an interview but not the job. What I did get was a kindly letter from the Head of News listing all the questions about Glasgow and Scotland I couldn't answer, with some facts and figures that I had omitted to research! I cannot tell you how embarrassing it all was. I had no clue as to the football teams, or the population figures, etc., etc.

But I did learn from my mistakes and several months later I got an interview at the rival commercial radio station in Edinburgh. I did all my research about the city as thoroughly as a black cab driver would learn the Knowledge for London. I went to the interview armed with information, rather than not knowing enough, and wasn't asked a single question I'd planned on (isn't that called Sod's Law?) but felt much more confident in the interview situation and got the job!

Let's look at the your checklist:

- What's the job description?
- How well qualified are you for the job?
- What are your assets?
- What might get in the way of doing the job well?
- Any outside experiences or interests that might contribute to the post on offer?
- What type of responsibilities are involved?
- What about the salary? What are your realistic expectations of this?
- Any travel or accommodation issues?
- If you're a parent, what's the company's attitude towards working parents?
- Will this job work for you?
- Why should they pick you?

The interview

So you've got the interview and now you have to do your best on the day. Preparation includes researching what you're going to wear. Dress appropriately and in clothes that you are going to feel comfortable in and not something that will make you feel out of place. On the basis that we form 90 per cent of our opinion about someone within the first 90 seconds of meeting them, your appearance will represent a large part of the impression you create when you walk through the door for a job interview.

The answer in a situation like this is to dress appropriately for the occasion. If it's business, look businesslike. Even if you are a very flamboyant personality, don't overdo the flamboyant look. Be yourself but in the context of the professional situation. If you prance in with bright purple hair and thigh-length boots, you might just give the wrong impression.

It sounds so obvious but we all want to present ourselves in the best possible light and in a short space of time get our personality across. While it is important to show our individuality and uniqueness, it is also about coming over as a team player. Someone who will fit in yet make a unique difference. So unless you're going for a job as a performance artist, think about the context in which you're hoping to work. There is simply nothing worse than turning up for any interview and feeling out of place. Your focus of attention will rapidly shift from the interview itself to feeling uncomfortable and, at worst, wanting to go and hide under the nearest stone!

We have already discussed body language but this is a great time to try out your new and revised gestures when confronted with a potentially nerve-racking situation. It's important that you light up the room when you walk in, so enter with a smile on your face and looking confident. Good eye contact and, if the opportunity arises, a firm handshake will make a difference.

Every non-verbal gesture says a great deal in a short space of time about who you are. How you stand, sit and look contribute to the overall impression you are making on the person or people interviewing you. Sit upright rather than leaning back in your chair or leaning in too closely. Remember, do not cross your arms, as this could look like a defensive or nervous gesture. Don't wring your hands or play with your rings or jewellery. Open gestures display an open personality and will help you give a more relaxed interview.

And you can afford to be relaxed or even enjoy the process if you have done your homework. In fact you can actively look for opportunities to promote yourself in terms of your personal qualities and professional qualifications. If there is a chance for an anecdote or a mention of your life outside the workplace that might help portray you as an interesting and well-rounded character, make sure you get that information out there.

We will look separately at listening skills and how essential the art of listening is to the whole process of communication. It is just as vital in an interview situation. Although you are bound to be feeling a little nervous, it is important to listen to what you are being asked so that you make the most of your reply. There is a difference between selling yourself and overloading your prospective employers with too much irrelevant information.

Remembering to breathe is important. Holding your breath is a natural reflex action to being scared. Breathing deeply brings you back to present time and helps you to feel much more in control of the situation. Fake it to make it. In any situation where we want to promote ourselves in the best possible light, it is natural to feel nervous. But if you can come over as a relaxed and confident person, even if you have got butterflies in your stomach, you will see how well your interviewers respond to your calm attitude, and that in turn will help you to unwind and become so involved in your interview that you banish all fears, projections and worries about what they might be thinking of you and whether you do or don't get the job.

Think about what you're saying and listen to the other person and you can fool yourself you're in an enjoyable and interesting conversation with somebody else, rather than being acutely aware that you're desperate to get the job over and above the other 500 applicants!

The main areas in a job interview will obviously be concerned with your professional skills and where you can match the job description. Interviewers these days are on the lookout for leadership skills and self-motivated people. Other qualities they will be seeking will be your ability to show initiative, diligence, team player and problem-solving skills, tenacity and the ability to work under pressure and deliver the goods. If you can think of some examples to back up these qualities, all to the good.

The other area you will need to have researched before your interview is the (almost) inevitable challenge of questions. They will almost certainly want to know why you want to work for them, why you left (or were asked to leave) your last company, or perhaps why you had difficulties with your last boss.

I am a great believer in the idea that there are no problems as such but opportunities to learn and grow. If you have been through a difficult ordeal in the workplace but gained something positive from the experience, then say that! It is a strength to admit to one's failings, especially if you have used situations to grow and change. That's a true sign of taking personal responsibility. Admit to being a human being! If you show you are a survivor, someone who learns from their experiences and has a good sense of humour to go with it, then you are making yourself into an attractive employee.

For many people today longterm periods of unemployment and age are both issues. Unfortunately ageism does exist, but remind youself that there are obviously advantages to being older. The older we are, the wiser we are, and we have a history of skills in the workplace. Mentoring, coaching and training skills are more of a feature in companies these days so, as an older candidate, as well as drawing on your strengths in terms of the amount of experience you have, you can also mention your skills in terms of helping younger employees. Other advantages about being older can be the lack of family ties, which means you are able to travel. This makes you adaptable and versatile.

There is a big emphasis on being multi-skilled. Older employees will have gained varied experiences in the workplace over the years, which may well stand them in good stead for the job they are applying for. When I went back to work as the mother of young children, I discovered that, far from being in my way, it stood me in good stead. I had become much more adaptable and an expert juggler. It also helped me to put work situations in perspective. I knew all about responsibility and caretaking. I believe that made me a better employee. Those caring skills that had been enhanced by parenting eventually led me into the field of training and coaching, coupled with an interest in self-development.

Which neatly leads onto another point. If you have self-awareness, that is a positive feature to display at your interview. With the growing interest in personal responsibility and leadership skills in the workplace, a healthy sense of self can mark you out from the rest of the field.

Obviously job interviews will vary but there are some basic categories. There is the one-to-one interview but that is less common, and most companies will have a panel of interviewers. If you know who they are before the day, that will help on the planning front. But it's important to establish the key person on the panel and address the different members appropriately. For example, the key interviewer may be your future boss so you would address that person regarding your skills and previous experience. There may be someone there from human resources who would be interested in your ability to work with a team or group of people – in other words your people skills. A manager may be interested in your questions about the company and what kind of profile you can help raise. It's all common sense but worth mentally preparing for before you arrive, so you come over as enthusiastic and interested rather than hesitant and awkward.

Sometimes people are asked for preliminary meetings in a social situation. Although in theory these are more relaxed and informal, the truth is you still need to know exactly who you are meeting up with and why they want to meet you. The answer of course is to be prepared but to come over as natural and spontaneous!

Paul is a 43 year old primary school headmaster, married with four children. Knowing him on a personal level, he's exactly the sort of person I would like to teach my three children. Enthusiastic, caring and motivated. With a very successful track record, Paul was an obvious candidate for promotion. He'd applied and failed to get four headships in other schools. He came for a voice-coaching session with me when he realised he was letting himself down at the interview.

'My presentations have been awful. Initially I was very nervous, obviously nervous. I had been aware of a tight throat and an inability to breathe normally. Because I had been nervous, I relied on using cue cards and reading the presentation. The professional feedback was that I had not been positive. One person said I wasn't convincing, another that I appeared to lack passion.

I know that I am generally good at relating to others and can communicate well on a one-to-one basis. I can also tell a good story in assembly. But when I went for a voice-training session and practised reading my presentation, I noticed that the very act of reading served to cut off real communication between Joanna and myself. I also realised how off-putting this must have been for the people interviewing me.

Joanna talked me through the techniques of using the voice. To sit with both feet on the ground and to be aware of my voice coming from my stomach. This helped me to find the full range of my voice. More importantly, Joanna helped convince me that I have the natural ability to present well and that this was something I was doing on a daily basis in school. It was revelation to know that the answer lay inside me and it was just a matter of relaxing and being myself. It has put on the road to discovering my true voice and learning to express myself in an authentic and real way.'

Footnote: since this was written, Paul has got a job as a headteacher.

MEDIA INTERVIEWS

We'll come on to general media interviewing skills later in this chapter, after looking at the specifics of each medium you are dealing with. The basis for any media interview goes back to the five Ws discussed in the Media section (p. 71):

- What
- Why
- Who
- Where
- When

That should form the basis of any story. While there are essential differences between the different media, one thing they all have in common is the fact that they either want a story from you or an opinion about a story they are running. So you need to be armed with your facts and opinions, having researched any difficult areas that you think may arise.

Once you can answer the five Ws in terms of the story you are going to tell, you've got a very good foundation from which to work. This in essence is your message. The journalist doesn't need to know every detail of your life, but do think of stories and points you can make to illustrate what you're saying.

Newspaper and magazine interviews

Planning and preparation is as essential for a newspaper interview as it is for any other. You need to know what your message is and have prepared for all eventualities before you meet up with the reporter.

Some key points for print interviews are:
- Research the newspaper or magazine's coverage – what's the audience?
- Plan your message.
- Never say anything 'off the record'; it may well end up in print.
- Never give 'yes' or 'no' answers to the reporter's questions; you may well find that their question becomes your direct quote.
- Make sure that what gets into print is your story not the reporter's
- Beware of saying anything that could be contentious unless you make it clear is your personal opinion – you don't want the lawyers after you.

- Keep a record of what you've said, just in case something ends up on the front page that you're not happy with.
- You can always ring the journalist after the interview and check they are happy with the information you gave them and see if they need anything else.
- Establish yourself as a useful contact.

Author and print journalist Jane Alexander has some excellent tips on giving a good interview.

'What does a journalist want from an interview? Well, that depends on the journalist and the publication. But I can tell you what I want, which is pretty simple. First of all, I'm hoping for a pleasant encounter, a friendly exchange, a sense of connecting at some point, however fleeting. Believe it or not, the vast majority of journalists aren't out to rook you – they simply want a good story. So help them out.

Secondly I'm looking for a fresh, exciting, informative and newsworthy interview. I want answers to obvious questions and hopefully some surprises too. I want to be entertained so that I, in turn, can write an entertaining, exciting piece.

I've interviewed a lot of people, including many famous people, in my time and some of the most famous were the most boring. If you really can't be bothered to rise above 'yes' and 'no' answers, then don't do the interview. However, if you do want some kind of meaningful exchange, here are a few tips.

It's well worth figuring out the kind of questions the journalist will ask and pre-paring some answers, at least in rough format. If there are areas you don't want to cover, that's fine, but don't come across as precious or tantalising. Obviously, if your main claim to fame is that you're some famous actress's personal trainer, you're going to be asked about X. If you can't answer that kind of question, it's only fair to tell journalists that before the interview.

Try to make complicated theories or ideas simple. However, have the back-up science at your fingertips in case the journalist is technically minded and needs more. There's nothing more irritating than waffle or airy-fairy flannel.

Try, if you can, to think in sound-bites. Short pithy sentences make great quotes. As do funny or slightly outrageous asides. Above all, get your personality across. It's great to tell anecdotes but make sure they're relevant; don't drone on for ages. There's nothing worse than the interviewee who's in love with their own voice and meanders through their life story when all you want is a couple of lines about their latest film.

Do feel free to add in anything you think the journalist has missed – in a tactful way. It's fine to gently ask what they thought about such and such a point. Asking questions in return (in an interested way, not an interrogation) is also a great way of bonding with someone – and most journalists feel warm and fluffy if someone shows interest in them (and are more likely to give you a good review/write-up). Always finish the interview by asking if there is anything else they need – and giving them the opportunity to get back in touch in case they think of anything else they would like to ask or check. If you don't want to give out your phone number that's fine – offer an email or suggest they go via your agent or another third party.'

Radio interviews

Generally speaking you are more likely to be approached by the radio station looking for an interview. Unless of course they are responding to your press release or to some information you have contacted them with.

If they contact you by telephone and ask you to do an interview there and then, always ask for ten minutes or so to prepare. It can be downright dangerous to launch into an 'on-air' conversation without any preparation. If you do that you are far more likely to be caught unawares and say something you may regret later. As with any interview situation, make sure you have had the preparation time you need.

Always prepare for the worst-case scenario or the hostile questions. Even if the subject you are talking about is not controversial, you may discover during the interview that the reporter's done their research and come up with something potentially contentious from your past! If, for example, you have ever appeared in the press in a less than favourable way in the past, capitalise on the situation, as I managed to do in the example below.

I spent a day doing media training with a racehorse trainer turned breeder. He had come to me because he had had a rough time with the press in the past about some scandal in the racing world. Although he had not been seriously implicated, he had suffered at the hands of the media and the experience had left him feeling nervous about any interviews he might have to give with the launch of his new career.

I managed to convince him that any airtime opportunity is a good one. It's a chance for an individual or organisation to promote themselves or their work. If the hostile question comes up (and in this case it was going to be inevitable), a planned answer can have some positive results!

We spent the day practising his interviews with a tape recorder. The advantage of that, of course, was that he could listen to himself and hear how he came over. At first it was obvious he was very hesitant about the past being raked up, but by the end of the day he had been able to master the art of acknowledging the question but giving the answer he wanted. For example: 'Yes, that was a difficult time in my life. But looking back I see it was an opportunity for me to learn and benefit from the experience. Thanks to that time I have now been able to…'

Never sound defensive or hostile. It just makes you sound guilty! Answer the question just to keep the reporter happy, but then you can use it as a launchpad to say what benefits you and your company have experienced as a result of that time. I have to say by the end of the session the client was much more confident about his future press appearances because he had researched, prepared and practised what he was going to say even in the most difficult of circumstances.

If you are doing an interview for a radio news bulletin, again do your research by listening to their output before you go to the interview. These days radio journalists will usually use a 7-15-second clip of your interview packaged between their voiceover. If they use your answer or interview in its entirety, then that is a little different. But each story is generally given anything from 30 seconds to a minute and a half. Not long to get your message across.

So be clear and confident. It is important to sound interested and interesting. If you sound dull, or bored by what you're saying, you are not going to hook in the interviewer or the audience. Sounding enthusiastic, passionate and engaged is what brings your interview and your story to life. Appropriate language is essential. It's no good using learned and complex terms when your radio listener wants to understand clearly and simply what you are saying.

Radio is not only a transient medium but also a non-visual one. So you have to make what you say sound vivid and full of bright colours, an interesting picture, rather than meaningless, dull and insipid. You should sound as though you are engaged in conversation and not reading from a book. The written word is different from the conversational. It is vital we remember that in broadcast situations.

Your aim is to get your message across. It won't come across if you use flowery language or jargon, or make the assumption that your audience knows what you're talking about. Sounding conversational and natural makes it easy for the listener to understand what you're saying. Keeping them hooked in and listening is your goal. It's the KISS factor – keep it simple, stupid!

For radio, you will either be interviewed on location, in the radio studio, down the line or over the telephone. When you go into the radio studio, there is likely just to be you and the presenter or reporter. You may be in the main studio where the programme is being transmitted or in a voice booth.

You are usually asked to say a few words so that the journalist can test the level of your voice. Don't worry. The standard question will be 'What did you have for breakfast?' I can't say I know the origins of this banal question, but the ridiculous thing is I have sometimes witnessed interviewees getting worked up about what to answer. Perhaps they think what they had for breakfast is some kind of barometer of their intelligence, or has a deep and hidden meaning about them as a potential interviewee! Often the answer will be 'nothing' and that is not enough to check the level of your voice. So you could plan to talk about your exotic breakfast in advance and you will not be caught out on that one!

Do not be intimidated by the microphone, it's important to remember the interviewer is a real person and to keep good eye contact. Don't rush. Take a breath after they have asked you a question, so that you can ensure you have really understood what you are being asked. Rushing into the answer can cause problems in the editing process and it might mean you end up saying something you didn't really intend to. It is important not to interrupt the interviewer or talk over anyone else, because it is impossible to hear what is said through a babble of voices. This is also a good thing to remember as it will encourage you to take breaths and pauses.

Talk at a slower pace than you would do normally so that you stay in control of what you are saying. Don't take copious bits of paper into a radio interview. There is nothing worse than hearing paper rustling. Also it is a complete distraction for you if you constantly have to keep looking down at your notes. It will mean you are not responding to the interviewer and you will more than likely lose track of what you're trying to say.

Hopefully your research and preparation beforehand mean you know what you want to say and the points you want to get across. If necessary, write a few bullet points down on a postcard for an emergency situation, but hang onto the fact that you have been wheeled in either because it's your story or because you are an expert on the subject under discussion.

You know your story better than anyone. So if it's the first time someone else has heard it, keep it simple not complex, and speak in a way that they're going to hear and understand first time round. It's probably the only chance they will get to hear it.

Whether your radio interview is live or recorded, I always tell people I train to perform as if it's live. You only have one chance to get your point across. If you keep having 'another go' at 'getting it right' your interview can sound stale or boring. Having said that if you make a mistake, live or pre-recorded, it is important to let the interviewer know you are not happy with your answer – especially if what you have just said can be misinterpreted. It is easy for any interviewer to rewind or start the question again. If it is 'live' then it is perfectly acceptable to correct yourself on air. For example you might say, 'Let me make it clear…'.

If you go for an interview with a major organisation like the BBC, it is a possible you will be in a remote studio where there may only be you and the microphone and no presenter in front of you. Do not let this put you off. You are always talking to someone. You just have to imagine Doris or Derek in front of you!

Television interviews

There was a time when many people would have shied away from doing television interviews or thought it unlikely they would ever be asked to do one. But with the ever-expanding world of television, and with the public's access to that world greater than ever, it is always a good idea to be prepared. It is no longer the privilege of the chosen few to appear on the small screen. Whatever walk of life you're in, there is always a possibility you may be asked to be interviewed for television. And if you haven't been asked you may well want that window of opportunity to promote yourself or your business.

Whenever I do training with groups of people such as civil servants, or those employed in the public sector, I warn them that they can no longer hide away from the cameras. It is more and more common to call on those 'on the ground' who can talk with real authority and experience about what's going on. Often the higher up the ladder the manager or team leader is, the further away they are from what's going on on the ground.

Of course the thought of being interviewed for television can be a frightening one if you have never done anything like that before. But in truth it is exactly the same as being interviewed for any other medium. If you are prepared for what lies ahead and have covered all eventualities, it is difficult to go wrong. I know I've said this before but the truth is no one can make you say anything you don't want to. If you've got your information, facts, stories and tactics for answering the more difficult questions, you will not fail. Preparation is the key.

Having said that, there are some obvious differences between radio and television. One is the visual element, and what you wear is important. If radio is about sound then television is about visuals. Always be aware of the picture and how you appear in front of camera. There is no doubt that what the audience sees is how they'll judge your contribution. In other words you never get a second chance to create a first impression. If the viewer is distracted by what you're wearing they are less likely to hear what you're saying.

There are a few 'no's in television in terms of dress! First rule is don't wear anything that might strobe on camera. So leave that hound's tooth check jacket or the highly checked tie in the wardrobe. Avoid heavily spotted or striped clothes and don't be tempted to wear all black, because too much black doesn't do you any favours. Equally, white can look great with a jacket, but sometimes bright white on its own can glare. However foolish you may feel, do ask the producer before you go on television if there is anything you should avoid wearing. If you are really organised, you can check out the colour of the television set or backdrop so that you can match up your clothes! Sometimes there are technical reasons why people shouldn't wear a particular colour, and in my experience journalists and producers can sometimes, under pressure, forget to pass that information on to the potential interviewee.

For a few years I worked on a series of documentaries where we filmed reconstructions. This often involved the interviewee giving his or her interview with the reconstruction being shown behind them. To do this we had to use what's known as a chromakey screen. These are usually green or blue. In our case we always had this blue screen and, for technical reasons that were quite beyond me, if our interviewees wore anything blue, the reconstruction would end up plastered all over the blue in their clothes rather than on the screen behind them. And sometimes, despite our best intentions, there were occasions when we might have passed on the information to the organisation we were working with but they had forgotten to tell their interviewee to wear any colour other than blue.

I remember well a hysterical incident where we had police and firemen changing into each others' clothes in a small corridor because they'd turned up in blue. That's all very well if you can rely on finding a stranger who wears the same size clothes as you do. Once again a case of forewarned is forearmed!

In broadcasting generally, but particularly in television, it is the immediacy of the communication that matters. As an interviewee, you are both informing and performing at the same time, so it's important to be well briefed without sounding under pressure, and relaxed without appearing uninterested. These things come with practice. Learn to be comfortable with your delivery, the sound of your own voice and how you appear.

Remember that television has a tendency to exaggerate any mannerisms you may have unconsciously picked up. While it is important to be animated, repeated hand-waving or other odd gesticulations are best left to some of our more eccentric broadcasters. Unusual or repetitive mannerisms can be distracting and even irritating to viewers.

On the other hand, appearing too laid back can give the impression that you are bored. It's up to you find the balance that suits you but, broadly speaking, when you have a point to make, do so clearly and assertively, and when someone else is talking, concentrate on them and what they're saying.

Words are used to communicate information and to relate or express an experience. Be mindful of what you're trying to say and to whom and in what circumstances. The best advice is to play it straight from the start. Don't try to cut across other guests or the presenter when they're speaking. If the focus is not on you then your microphone will usually be faded down. What might strike you as a funny one-liner may be broadcast as an inaudible comment off-camera which will only confuse the viewer. Even if it's very funny and has the television crew laughing out loud, if the audience has missed it will simply serve as an annoyance to them.

Television journalists work to programme and bulletin deadlines. As with radio, interviews are either conducted in a studio or on location. But there are different mediums within this context:

- Phone interview
- On location
- Live link
- Remote studio
- Manned studio

1. Phone interview

Don't take it for granted that if you are asked to do an interview, especially a news interview, you will actually be appearing on television. Because more and more organisations are offering either hourly bulletins or even continuous news coverage, journalists are looking for an immediate response, particularly if it's a breaking story. The quickest way is to record a telephone interview, which will be broadcast either over a still photograph of the interviewee or a generic image.

If you are being asked to do a phone interview (sometimes referred to as a phono) make sure you understand what the issue is that you are being asked to react to. Establish whether the interview will be live or recorded. If it is recorded then there is a good chance the interview will be edited, so it is important to be very clear what you have to say. Try to keep your answers concise, not more than thirty seconds. This is known as a 'sound bite'.

If the interviewer's questions are not leading to the answers you want to give, be confident enough to direct the interview your way. You can do this in a number of ways but the easiest is to preface what you have to say with something like: 'There is another important point …'; 'I think there is something some people will be missing here …'; 'That's true, but in my opinion …'; 'In my experience …'; or 'Some people might say that, but personally I feel …'.

2. On location

The same rules apply. Make sure you know what you want to say and what the main issues are. Check whether the interview is live or recorded. 'On location' will usually mean at an office or in a commercial environment. This time of course you will be in vision, so your appearance is important. Make sure it's appropriate for the occasion. Make sure it reflects the image you want to project – for example, working executive, prosperous business-person, or media smoothie!

Remember that if the interview is recorded it will be edited. This gives you more control over the finished item. If you feel you have made a mistake – for example mispronounced a name, quoted the wrong figures or lost the thread of what you were trying to say – you can stop the interview and retrace your steps.

In fact, it's very important to know you have this level of control in any interview situation – even if it's live. If you feel what you've said may be misinterpreted or you have been unclear, you can either ask the journalist to repeat the question or, if it's a live situation. say something along the lines of: 'Let me just make that clear, what I mean is …'. Most interviewers will be happy to oblige. After all they want to look professional too.

Don't wait until the interview is over. Remember production time is expensive and the crew may be running short of time. You may be fobbed off with assurances that they'll 'edit round the problem'. They may – or they may not. Either way that decision is out of your hands, so it's best to stop and correct the situation immediately.

Finally check the background for the interview is appropriate. It won't do your image any good if you're standing in front of an advertising hoarding that says 'Is this the sort of person you would trust?' Exaggerated, you may think, but what you're standing in front of is important. How many times have you seen plants or foliage seeming to sprout out of someone's head?

3. Live link

A live link gives you less control over the situation. You will be speaking directly to the interviewer on location or to a presenter in the studio. There will be a limited amount of allocated time, so it is even more important in this case that you are confident with your information. There will also be less opportunity to have a rerun at what you wish to say.

If you are speaking to an interviewer in a studio, you may not be able to see the person you are talking to. You are usually given an ear-piece so you can hear what is being said. Direct your answers straight to the camera. Ignore anything else that is going on around you (unless it has a direct impact on the story!).

If you have any problems with the sound, tell the producer or a member of the crew on location immediately and they can adjust the levels. There's nothing worse than going on air and staring blankly at the camera while someone in the studio repeatedly asks 'Can you hear me? Can you hear me?'

4. Remote studio

Occasionally you may be asked to do an interview from a remote studio. This can be an unnerving experience. Remote studios are usually just big enough to accommodate a camera and a desk or chair. You may be contributing to a studio discussion hundreds of miles away but all you will see is the lens of the camera, which is operated automatically from the main studio. The only link which you have with what's going on is through your ear-piece.

Again, make sure you are happy with the sound levels before the interview starts. Listen very carefully to what is being said and deliver your interview straight to camera. Wait until you've been given clearance from the director that the item is over, before you leave. Unplugging and leaving an empty desk while still on air is not a good idea!

And remember that you may be on camera before the interview begins, so when the presenter introduces you or mentions your subject-matter, muster up a bright, breakfast smile just in case. It's important to be in 'presenter mode' from the minute you arrive on location or at the studio. so that a sneaky camera shot will not catch you unawares or present you in a way you are going to regret later!

5. Manned studio

This is the situation most people are familiar with, but initially it may seem quite intimidating being surrounded by a large number of people who all seem to know more about what's going on than you do.

If you are appearing on a programme (in other words something longer than a short interview on a new bulletin or news programme), you are likely to be taken to an area known as the Green Room. This gives you a chance to meet people directly involved with the programme you are going to appear on, and possibly other guests as well. You are normally well looked after in these circumstances, with refreshments provided and a chance for you to spend a few moments going through the key points of your imminent interview, which hopefully you planned earlier.

A live television interview for a major network broadcast organisation can be a stressful experience, but there are simple steps you can take to feel more comfortable and more in control. Go to the loo before you go to the studio! This will give you a chance to check your grooming and make-up. Asking for a drink of water when you arrive at the studio is important as well, to avoid dehydration.

If you are asked to do a studio interview 'As Live', it means the interview will be recorded as though it were live – all in one chunk – but transmitted at a later date. This affords you some of the control you have on a location interview but you won't be given more than two or three re-runs, as studio time is expensive. And I would urge you to always do your interviews as though you've only got one chance to do them. That means you will deliver your best, most focused interview first time round. My experience is that the more runs you have at an interview, the more jaded, bored and uninterested you are likely to sound.

There will be some reminders about interview techniques at the end of this section but let me remind you at this juncture of the importance of posture and body language when you are on screen.

Sit up straight and look the interviewer in the eye. Folding your arms or hunching over the desk can be interpreted as defensiveness on your part. Equally, looking overly relaxed may be interpreted as arrogance. Let common sense prevail. It is important that your message is not contradicted visually.

Be aware of the cameras at all times. Don't assume that because someone else is speaking, the cameras are not on you. Look at the interviewer and don't address the studio camera directly, as it looks unnatural and will confuse the viewer and possibly the interviewer.

Remember that studio staff are there to make sure the programme works and gets to air. If there's something you don't understand, then ask. If you feel you are being fobbed off, your point of contact is the floor manager. If you are still not happy you can speak to the producer. In extreme circumstances, if you are concerned you have been brought in to talk about something you can't comment on, or you have been misled in some way, then ask for the editor. It is very unlikely however that this type of situation will arise.

Media interview checklist

- Establish what the interview is really about.
- What's the format? Is it live, pre-recorded, in the studio?
- Make sure your appearance is appropriate.
- Ensure you have the correct facts and figures.
- Can you deliver information clearly in sound bites?
- If you realise you've made a mistake, correct yourself immediately.
- In a recorded situation, ask for a retake if you lose the plot.
- Emphasise the points you feel strongly about.

Steve Brodie is the BBC Home Affairs Correspondent for the South West. He specialises in investigative journalism, has worked for newspapers and radio and as a news editor for various organisations.

'Unless your are a dodgy politician, a crook, or a senior policeman attempting to explain why the crime figures are so bad, then you have nothing to fear from the TV or radio journalist. The electronic medium by its very nature wants to sound and look good. The journalists – the good ones – will go to every length to get a good clip, the 20 seconds which tell the story. It's up to the interviewee to be well prepared and clear in their mind what they want to say.

There is a major and fundamental difference between the newspaper or magazine reporter with his notebook and the radio or TV journalists with their mini-disc and imposing cameras. The old trick of the newspaper reporter, to put the 'victim' at ease and then say 'Isn't it true that some officers in the Met are corrupt and should be sacked', becomes in print, 'Today a leading member of the community says Met cops are corrupt'. That doesn't work on air – even if the interviewee agrees with the statement, the radio or TV journalist is unlikely to use the exchange because it doesn't make good radio or television.

Naturally the television journalist wants to get articulate answers –but they want passion and impact. What they do *not* want is over-scripted, over-considered replies. They are looking for honestly felt clips, in ordinary every-day language. The trick is not to try and be someone else. Be yourself and tackle the question or suggestion as you would in any normal conversation at home, in the workplace or in the pub. Above all don't go into great swathes of detail as there just isn't the time and it will never get to air. The main network news programmes are only thirty minutes long - you only have seconds to make your point, defend your position or argue your case.

Only programmes like *NewsNight* or Radio 4's *Today* look for more in-depth debate. But even here time is at a premium – if it's not to the point, interesting and topical, forget it. Be clear in your mind and then deliver with style!

No worthwhile journalist will ask one-word questions, and don't try to be clever in return, as a reply of just 'Yes' or 'No' is seldom used. Take the opportunity to reply 'Yes' and then give a brief concise answer.

Live or recorded interviews? Both have their advantages and disadvantages. If you are confident in your preparation and feel able to react, then take any offer of the 'Liver'. You will almost certainly get more time and be able to use the chance to get across your answer without the possibility of losing it in the edit. Remember, always ask the name of the presenter and the first question – you will always be told the former and usually the latter. There is of course always the danger of the slip of the tongue or having your ignorance found out ! The recorded interview gives you – and the journalist – the chance to cut out any mistakes, thus making a more rounded package. But remember, be to the point and concise. Rambling answers will be ignored.

Radio stations always prefer the quality interview. If you are offered the chance to go to a studio, then take it. Arrive on time and never rush into a studio. If you are interviewed over the phone at home, then select somewhere where you are comfortable – and turn off your own radio and TV.

Above all be yourself. I have lost count of the number of times I have arrived to interview quite senior people and had a perfectly acceptable conversation about how and what the interview is to be about, only to hear them reply in stilted cliché-ridden terms once the red light was on.

For good or ill television is the most powerful medium in the world - use it to your advantage.'

THE INTERVIEWING PROCESS

Answering clearly

One of the most common errors when being interviewed by the media is made by interviewees unaware of the difference between direct and indirect quotes. Don't be pressurised into giving 'Yes/No' answers, especially over the telephone. There's no guarantee that paraphrased opinions won't turn up directly attributed to you. An ill-timed yes or no answer may find you being directly quoted in a completely different way from how you might wish to express yourself.

For example:

Q: I've got a copy of your new survey that says the UK is the worst when it comes to customer care. One point to come out of this survey is that whilst some businesses like travel firms have done their best to improve customer care, professionals like solicitors come way down the list. Sounds as if some legal firms are living in the dark ages. Is that true?

A: Yes.

End Result: XX from XX believes British solicitors couldn't care less when it comes to customer care. He says: 'Legal firms are still living in the dark ages. When it comes to customer service they're the worst in Europe.'

Although strictly speaking it's not wholly inaccurate, it is clearly not what the interviewee said. Neither is the message delivered in the tone that is likely to improve family relations if your sister-in-law is a solicitor!

Let's run that one again:

Q: I've got a copy of your new survey that says the UK is the worst when it comes to customer care. One point I wanted to check was where you say that, while businesses like travel companies have done most to improve their customer service, some professionals like solicitors are among the worst. Sounds as if some legal firms are living in the dark ages. Is that true?'

A: Well, first of all it is a survey so it's not my personal view. It's the majority view of those people who were interviewed. Clearly many people believe that legal services are an area where customer relations can be improved. Larger companies like travel firms are finding that outsourcing their customer services to professionals like us allows them to concentrate on their business – confident that their client concerns are being handled promptly and efficiently.

Better end result: XX of XX believes that British solicitors could learn a lesson from other sectors when it comes to customer care. A survey by the company shows that lawyers are bottom of the league in Europe for customer services. Mr XX said: 'Larger companies like travel firms are finding that outsourcing their customer services to professionals like XX allows them to concentrate on their business, confident that their client concerns are being handled promptly and efficiently.'

- Beware of Yes and No answers.
- Don't be rushed into making incomplete answers.
- Always state clearly and fully what your answer is to individual questions, even if it means repeating or rephrasing the question directed to you.

Hostile interviews

You cannot be thrown by any interview situation if you have planned for every eventuality. Nobody can ever make you say anything you don't want to. Do not give your power away to the interviewer. It is important you stay in control of the message and not the other way round.

In every situation where clients have talked to me about being 'caught out', it has only been because they hadn't banked on the 'low ball' question hurtling their way. Remember your mental filing cabinet. File away those replies that will get you out of a potentially difficult situation. Never sound hostile or defensive. Acknowledge the question but turn the airtime you've been given to your advantage. Sounding angry only makes you look like you've got something to hide.

CORE SKILLS

Find your voice

Your voice is a wonderful tool. It's unique and it's you. Good presenting is about feeling good about your voice and your delivery. Most people will be aware that they sound different from the way they perceive themselves. Practising with a simple cassette recorder will go a long way to preparing you for broadcast work and ensuring you are focusing your attention on your script, questions or answers, rather than just how you sound. Being involved in what you're saying is a vital part of good delivery.

Just remembering to breathe makes a big difference. When we're nervous we tend to breathe in a more shallow way and that affects our voice and makes it sound strained. Before going on air, breathe deeply and relax, and prepare to enjoy yourself. It is so important to think of an interview as an enjoyable experience rather than some ordeal you have to get through.

Shallow breathing makes your voice sound high and thin. Good breathing calms you down, gives you time to think, and makes for much better delivery without even trying. Breathing from your stomach brings you into line with your feelings and, in a way relating to the whole of your being, helps your voice to sound fuller and richer. In essence, breathing from your centre helps you to feel more centred and in turn your voice will sound centred.

Vocal image

Your voice usually sounds quite different when you hear it back on tape and it's not always an accurate representation of what's going on. Having said that, it is useful to listen to your work and become aware of the areas you need to improve upon. Practice really does help us to become (more) perfect! Listen out for your pace, timing, inflection, diction, style and variation of tone depending on what you're presenting.

Go back to the image of a canvas. How many colours and how much depth we give our painting is reflected in the overall picture. The voice is just the same. The more energy and focus we put into our voice the richer and more resonant it will sound. The more likely our message will be heard. We can sound pleased, happy, enthusiastic, or we can give the impression of being uninterested, uncaring and casual when we don't think about what we're saying. A good voice can create wonderful pictures for the listener.

To speak well is about conveying your message to your audience. It's important to be yourself and to feel comfortable with how you're speaking. You don't have to copy anyone else, you just need to better your own performance or to brush up on areas you don't feel happy with. Be authentic! Your audience doesn't want an impostor or to hear a pseudo accent. They want to hear you.

Good sound

Good sound is the quality or tone of your voice – the timbre. It's also you and your individuality. Being over-controlled, or even forcing unnatural sounds out, doesn't work. What does work is being relaxed, breathing well and staying within your comfort zone.

That doesn't mean there isn't an element of stretching your voice and using it to its full potential. This can create tension, which has a paralysing effect on the whole of our bodies. Nervousness makes for shallow and rapid breathing which immediately changes the voice pattern. If you do suffer from nerves, then it might help to remember that you're only ever really talking to one person at a time. Remember too that mistakes are not the end of the world. Everybody makes them. See them as a learning experience, or at the very least be prepared to learn from them. You cannot afford the luxury of self-criticism during an interview situation or in a presentation, but by all means reflect afterwards on your performance.

Delivery

If you have no visual connection with your audience, the way you use your voice is very important. Practise your delivery so you become comfortable with how your voice sounds. Accents and dialects are only confusing or intrusive to the audience if *you* are uncomfortable with how you sound.

As you practise be aware of the following:
- Pace: about three words to a second.
- Tone : be aware of what you're saying and who you're saying it to.
- Pitch: use all of your voice so you sound centred and real.
- Pause: remember to breathe; a pause in the right place can add more than any words to your delivery.
- Project: your enthusiasm, concern, anger, humour, etc.
- Enunciate: every syllable. You don't want to mumble.

SUMMARY

Things to think about before the interview:
- Prepare as much as possible
- Who's listening to you and what are you trying to tell them?
- Plan for what you want to say but don't learn it verbatim. You can always have a postcard with some bullet points on as a prompt.
- Have a few stories or colourful facts up your sleeve.
- Know your subject well so you can speak spontaneously.
- Are you sounding friendly or frightening, or frightened?

During the interview:
- Be aware of what you're saying and how you're saying it..
- Are you keeping the audience's attention?
- Clear speech, good scripting, speed of delivery and timing are all important
- Remember you have something interesting to say.
- Slow down, take your time and try to enjoy your airtime.
- Think before you speak.
- Deliver what you have to say with confidence.
- Remember to pause; it gives you the chance to breathe, and your audience the chance to assimilate what you're saying.
- You can use repetition to drive home a point but avoid jargon.
- Keep good eye contact.
- Use humour carefully.
- Never swear in the studio or on the set.
- Never argue while the programme is on air.
- Never make gratuitous comments.
- Watch body mannerisms: don't fiddle with your watch, hair, clothes, etc., don't scratch or point, don't wring your hands or flail your arms about.

Coping with nerves:
- Remember everyone suffers from them, just make sure your nerves don't control you.
- Face up to your fears.
- Turn negative nerves into positive power.
- Practice kills panic – but don't learn your speech or presentation off by heart.
- Think positive thoughts and believe in yourself.
- Stay calm, appear confident, and smile!

8. LISTENING SKILLS
Learn to be Receptive

It might sound a contradiction in terms, but one of the best ways of finding your voice is to develop the art of listening.

While this book devotes a great deal of time to looking at ways in which to get our audience to listen to what we have to say, it is also crucial we understand what that audience wants. One of the key ways in which to give the right reply or deliver the right message is to be able to hear and understand what the other person has said or to comprehend their needs.

There truly is an art to listening. I am sure we have all had the experience at some time or another of being truly heard. Tuning in one hundred per cent to someone is a skill and one which we can all learn. In just the same way as we have to focus on what we want to say, we need to focus on what a person is saying to us. It's the difference between reading a book and realising you haven't taken in a word, or reading and absorbing every word of that page. How can you digest something if you haven't swallowed it in the first place?

It is so easy to tune out and not hear or not fully hear what the other person is saying. And that poor listening can lead to mixed messages and confusion. If you can focus your attention on the other person, you can see things from their viewpoint and it will help you to formulate and deliver the perfect answer. Communication is all about giving and receiving.

Clearly this is a two-way process and sometimes people can say something that is open to interpretation. But at least, if you're listening closely enough to have picked up the confusion, you can clarify what they mean.

Listening is considered so important that there is actually an international Listening Association. Browsing their website, I found lots of wonderful quotations about the art of listening. To me this summed it up: 'The most basic of all human needs is the need to understand and to be understood. The best way to understand people is to listen to them.' – Ralph Nichols

In a way listening to someone unconditionally is like giving them a massage. Being heard is therapeutic and boosts self-esteem and confidence. There are those people in the world who make you feel special, interesting and worthwhile. They have developed the art of listening.

Here are some tips for listening well:
- Make sure you can hear the person who's talking to you. You can't afford to be distracted by background noise or events.
- Have good eye contact.

- Put aside your judgements and be prepared to listen unconditionally.
- Really listen to what the person has to say. Don't start thinking about your response while they're still speaking.
- Don't interrupt! This really is one of the best ways to make the person feel put down and uninteresting. You will also come across as opinionated and rude. Besides which, if you wait for the person to finish, your interruption might well be irrelevant and you may come up with a more informed response.
- Be aware that if the speaker pauses, it could be for dramatic effect and to add weight to what they're saying. A pause does not mean a gap for you to charge in with an unwelcome reply!
- Stay focused and listening. You will pick up much more valuable information and if you do tune out you could well miss something you really need to hear.
- Try not to get caught in the trap of switching off when you hear something you don't agree with. You can present your reasoned argument later, when you have all the information and facts at your fingertips. There is nothing more frustrating for the person who's trying to say something than to have you telling them where they've got it wrong. You will come over as much more sincere, plausible and competent if you let them present their side of the argument first.
- It's also important not to make assumptions about what the other person has said.
- Be aware of your body language. Are you looking like you're listening? Are you making receptive gestures?
- You can tell a great deal about what's going on with the other person through their body language. Listen to their tone of voice and watch for the non-verbal signals that can sometimes tell you a great deal more about what they're saying than the actual words.

In my work as a journalist I have specialised in recent years in working with sensitive issues and interviewing victims of crime and abuse. It is my aim to get the best possible interview from them but I know that, if I don't put them at their ease or help them to feel comfortable in my presence, then they will find an already difficult situation even more difficult to handle. How I listen to them is critical.

If I look interested and empathetic, that helps build up the trust and rapport between us. In turn they will be more at ease and able to talk more freely. A great deal of that process with myself as interviewer is down to my ability to listen to them.

How many times have you heard a live interview when it seems the interviewer has failed to pick up on something quite crucial the speaker or interviewee has said? That's because they are too preoccupied with thinking about their next question, which they've written down or got firmly fixed in their head, rather than picking up spontaneously on what is actually happening.

If you're listening intently to someone it is possible to mentally summarise the important points they've made. If in doubt, check at an appropriate moment that you have heard them correctly. You can do this by feeding back what they've said in your own words. You can also ask them to expand on any point you're unclear about. Never be afraid to ask. I believe it's a sign of someone who's interested and keen to learn more. It's far better to get the facts straight or a clear understanding of what's been said, before launching into what might turn out to be an inappropriate response.

There's a useful technique described in the *The Complete Idiot's Guide to Clear Communication*, by Kris Cole – it's the acronym EARS:
E stands for exploring by asking questions
A is affirm to show you're listening
R is reflect your understanding
S is for silence.

Affirmative listening means we are showing the person who's speaking that we are listening through our non-verbal communication - in other words, our eye contact and gestures.

Reflection is when we feed back to the person what they have said but in our own words. It is also gives the speaker the chance to make sure his message has been understood clearly.

Silence: after you have said your piece, pause to see what the speaker has to say about your response.

What gets in the way of being a good listener? Feelings can distract us, so that it's hard to give our full attention to someone else. It's important not to act on our feelings without thinking them through. The art of unconditional listening is to be present and not to get distracted by random thoughts or feelings.

It's also important not to get caught up in the talker's feelings. If something the other person says creates a major emotional reaction in you, it's worth noting because that's going to be useful for you to consider at some point, but don't get distracted by it.

One person who has learned a great deal about the art of unconditional listening throughout her colourful and varied life is Jean. She is a 70-year-old retired hotelier, dentist, counsellor, mother of four, and grandmother of six, who extols the healing art of listening.

'"Be good and be quiet! Children should be seen and not heard!" We are intelligent beings so of course we learn to stay out of trouble when we hear this kind of admonition. We become quiet, shy, frustrated – or downright furious and throw tantrums, and all because we need to talk. We are the only species which has this ability and the only species which has feelings that get hurt, and the two are connected, we can recover from the hurt by talking.

Think of a young child who falls and hurts herself. She instinctively looks for someone to comfort her. She may cry or talk about what happened and will continue for as long as it takes to recover from the hurt, then the sun comes out and she is off to more exciting things.

Unfortunately there are rarely people around to listen. And even more rarely to listen for as long as we need to talk. We try talking to our teddy but it's not the same, and eventually we resign ourselves to the apparent fact that no one is interested in me, just the way I am. So – being intelligent – I learn I had better pretend that I am different, and be whatever others are interested in, because more than anything I need attention. Isn't this how we became good at that subject taught by the teacher we liked, chose the job we were good at, the partner who approved or fancied us?

So, if we all need to be listened to in order to reclaim our true intelligent interesting confident selves, where are we to find the listeners? Given the perfect listener, talking comes naturally and the floodgates open. We feel so much better for being listened to, but what about the listener? Unless the listener also gets a fair share of the attention, she will start avoiding us and we lose our perfect listener. The answer is to become a perfect listener ourselves, then teach others to listen to us.

A good listener is interested in me, and what has made me the way I am. Knowing that, given my circumstances, I have always done the very best I could and therefore deserve only admiration and respect. I know that is true of you and therefore it has to be true of everyone, including me, and this makes me a good listener. If anything gets in the way of our knowing this about ourselves, we need to find a friend and tell them about it, until we can see clearly that we were not to blame. Once we can leave behind the fear of blame or criticism our worlds open up.

A good listener is never critical, knows the talker is the only one who has the answer to their situation, and is willing to listen with respect and encouragement; delighting as the talker reclaims their own voice.'

9. PERSONAL LIFE
Apply your Skills

You may have thought this book was not for you because you are not planning to make that all-important speech at a family event, or host a presentation in the workplace, or even be put in front of the television cameras.

Not true. We all have a need and a right to be heard, and a right to have our say. In my experience as a broadcaster, trainer and mother of three, it is crucial to find your voice in any situation.

FINDING YOUR PERSONAL VOICE

This book is not just for people who want to find their voice in a professional situation. It's for anyone in any situation who needs to find their voice within. To say what they really want to say not what they think they should say. To find more effective and empowering ways of communicating with others.

A very well-know quotation from Nelson Mandela's inauguration speech when he became President of South Africa in 1994 turns up in many books these days because it is so inspirational and true:

'Our deepest fear is not that we are inadequate. Our deepest fear is that we are powerful beyond measure. It is our light, not our darkness that most frightens us. We ask ourselves 'Who am I to be brilliant, gorgeous, talented, fabulous?' Actually, who are you not to be? You are a child of God. Your playing small doesn't serve the world. There's nothing enlightened about shrinking so that other people won't feel insecure around you. We are all meant to shine, as children do … and as we let our light shine, we unconsciously give other people permission to do the same. As we're liberated from our own fear, our presence automatically liberates others.'

I believe FEAR lies behind many of our personal limitations. It's our lack of self-belief that can hold us back and stop us from achieving our highest potential, whether it's at home or in the workplace, or even in our relationships. Fear can be behind our not daring to speak up in any given situation.

Think of fear as standing for: False Evidence Appearing Real. There is some truth in the theory that if you worry or fear something enough, you can make your thoughts become a reality. But fear is only a projection of what might happen in the future and doesn't have to become a real life event!

Michaela is a single parent and studying law at university. She is keen to find her true voice so that when the time comes for her to stand up in court and deliver, she can do so confidently and assertively. Before her session with me started, Michaela recounted a significant and recurring dream she'd had which was directly connected to her voice and her inability to speak out in certain situations.

'In the dream, I am always going up in a lift. I can feel it rising, slowly and steadily. I can hear the gentle humming sound and see and feel the textures of the walls, the carpet and the mirrors. So I am going up and up nice and slowly. Then the lift stalls, jolts slightly, and there's silence. Absolute silence. For a split second. Then pure fear kicks in.

The lift is plummeting down, travelling at a horrific speed. The awesome power of gravity is so evident. There is an eerie silence in the lift except for the whistling sound outside that it makes as it speeds down the empty shaft. The force is so strong and I am unable to move. Every muscle is contracted and every nerve on end. My legs are like lead, my heart is in my mouth and I am paralysed by the profound sensation of falling.

Desperate, I want to scream. I am trying to scream. My mouth is wide open and I'm ready to scream for my life but my voice is paralysed. No voice, totally powerless and paralysed with fear.'

With the help of an analyst, Michaela had come to see that the one place in her body where she held all her tension was in her throat. It's also her weak spot physically, and if she's run down, overtired or anxious then that's the area where the physical problems are. She says her scream dream was about her inability, and yet her need, to scream in reality. Michaela says the dream was symbolic of her wish to communicate and make herself heard. This is how she describes her first voice training session.

'One gem I learned which struck me as the most important piece of advice was to think about and understand whatever it was I was reading out loud. All too often I read words off a page without thinking about what it actually means or even hearing it myself. If I can't hear it, how can I expect the listener to hear it? Or even a person I'm having a conversation with.

Slowing down and understanding the importance of slowing down, coupled with using my voice from my stomach rather than my throat. Wonderful stuff! I will take this into my everyday life. After my session I felt I knew some of my strengths and weaknesses and that I had discovered a part of my voice I didn't know existed.'

It's back to the inner talk issue. How we talk to ourselves on the inside has a tremendous impact on what happens on the outside. Our inner talk can be based on the negative beliefs we hold. These beliefs may come from our childhood, when criticisms or unfair judgements hurt us and stayed with us. We can be so tough on ourselves. Self-doubt is natural, but we have to learn to be able to praise ourselves as well as criticise. There is a link between our thoughts, feelings and behaviour. For example, fear can feel real but it is not reality. Negative self-talk and feeding off our fears can lead to negative expectations, and those expectations in turn can lead to a negative result.

Learn to be constructive in your criticism and be able to approve of your achievements and progress. Become aware of what you say to yourself. Drop the 'cant's' and 'wont's' and change the negative words to positive. So instead of 'I'm not good at', turn it to 'I'm good at'… I like the phrases, 'act as if' or 'fake it to make it'. Although it's not always easy even to pretend to believe in ourselves, just having a go at it can boost our confidence and make a real difference to what we do.

One of the great ways of not dealing with issues is avoidance. It is so much easier to bury or hide a problem, or dismiss it as irrelevant, than to face it and deal with it. Often that's because we fear that the process of dealing with it is going to be painful and harm us. But in my experience we can do ourselves far more harm by not confronting issues. It's the book of stamps syndrome (p. 13). We go on saying yes to everything when we really want to say no; taking on too much and feeling resentful but not knowing how to stop it happening. And then guess what, the last stamp of resentment goes in the book and we lose it. Everyone around is incredulous and cannot understand why we have over-reacted to a situation. But of course we are not just over-reacting to that one situation. It's also to the thousands of other things that have gone before it and the lid's finally blown off.

One of the ways in which we drive ourselves to limits that are not always realistic is the result of our need to be perfect. The human condition dictates that we can't be perfect, that we're here to learn our lessons through our imperfections. Try and see life's challenges as a chance to change for the better; an opportunity to grow and develop. It's easy to look back on situations and see how we might have done things differently; more productive to use the next similar scenario as a chance to put our new found awareness to the test.

RIGHTS AND RESPONSIBILITIES

We live in a world where we often see the blame game being played out. Somebody passing the buck and not wanting to take personal responsibility. It's a game that lacks integrity and doesn't help us to find our true voice. Finding our voice, in the truest sense of the phrase, means to speak our truth. Sometimes that's a scary thing to do because we're not colluding with everyone else and we are willing to take a stand.

That is not always easy and not always popular but one guarantee is that we will feel proud of ourselves and know on some profound level we our self-respect and integrity is intact.

We all have the right to be heard and have our say. We also have the right to think what we think and feel what we feel. But we have to remember that our personal response to situations is just that – a personal response. We can only say what's going on for us and not assume we know what's happening for someone else. So how you address a situation is important. Make sure the listener knows it is your feeling and not a feeling being imposed on them. We all need to have our feelings listened to.

Also, what about your needs? Well, they are your responsibility. If you don't tell someone what your needs are, or even acknowledge them to yourself, then you are not likely to get them met. Often we can be so busy rushing around meeting everyone else's needs that we completely forget to meet our own. And if we're not careful we can then slip into believing it's someone else's fault.

We all have rights, but there are also responsibilities to be met. Again it is up to us to decide how far our responsibilities go and when we might be at risk of robbing someone else of their responsibilities. It is very easy to think of caring as a virtue but, if we spend too much time caring for others, we not only neglect ourselves but we also take away the chance for that person to learn to take responsibility.

As parents of course we have responsibilities to our children. But surely it is also important to teach them how to grow into responsible adults – responsible for themselves as well as others. It's finding the balance. It's about compromise.

WORK-LIFE BALANCE

With more and more pressures put on us by today's society, it seems very hard to get that work-life balance right. Most of us need to work to live. But should we live to work? Certainly current thinking deems that we should go with the flow. In other words do what we're good at and stop struggling to do what doesn't come naturally. If you're a great artist, then paint. If you've got a wonderful voice, then sing. If you love words and literature, then write.

I know it isn't always that simple but we have to feed our soul and be inspired at least in some part of our life. Life has to have meaning. It gives purpose and focus to what we do. There has to be some point to what we're doing, otherwise it is literally pointless. Seeing the bigger picture or believing that life presents us with opportunities to change and grow is purposeful. If there is no direction to our lives it is much harder to be motivated and inspired. Finding your voice to get the life you want is a challenge for us all and brings into play that eternal quest to get the work-life balance right.

Goals

It's important to have goals because they give us direction and a path to follow. Setting our sights on something and then achieving it gives us our self-esteem a lift. It's an adrenaline boost.

Personally I find the relentless daily tasks can get to me – they can be so boring! The endless loads of washing, shopping, cooking, ironing (or not) and juggling kids, work, relationships. In other words Life. But I try to remember that there is a sense of enjoyment and fulfilment in every task I undertake and it's serving a purpose. If I spent every minute wishing away routine tasks, I would be wasting so much of my life thinking negatively!

When my third child was a baby and her brother and sister were at school there was the odd momentous occasion when I found I had read and finished a novel. It made me feel so good, so content, so fulfilled, and I just couldn't work out why. Then I realised it was about completing something. Finishing a task. And during that time of my life particularly, everything seemed a constant round of unfinished tasks. It was a very satisfying feeling, a bit like achieving our aims.

In my coaching sessions I always encourage individuals to set themselves a commitment – either a work or a personal one. Although I know it is important that we do things for ourselves, there's nothing like someone else setting us a challenge so that we have that sense of obligation to fulfil it!

Action plans may sound boring but they work. Committing to paper our plans and dreams for the future is somehow helping to bring them closer to reality. Imagine them – image them in – to your life and start taking steps towards achieving them. You will be surprised at the momentum your dreams take on and how they become reality.

Another great quotation comes from the American novelist John Gardner: 'There is something I know about you that you may not even know yourself. You have within you more resources of energy than have ever been tapped, more talent than has ever been exploited, more strength than has ever been tested and more to give than you have ever given.'

You need to learn to be discerning. There is a theory that some people are like drains, others like radiators; people who tend to be takers, others by nature givers. Drains are those who can leave you feeling quite exhausted and lacking in energy. Radiators are those people who make you feel uplifted and energised.

THERAPY

Often what we don't say can be as telling as what we do say. Lyn Macnab is an integrative counsellor and psychotherapist who works with clients in a way that respects their whole experience of life: mind, body and spirit. She is very interesting on the value and paradox of the role of the voice in the therapeutic context.

'Telling our story can be one of the most liberating and healing experiences in our lives, particularly when it is listened to carefully. As an experienced counsellor and psychotherapist I hear the most touching and profound stories that people have experienced. In using the word 'story', I am not in any way judging or trivialising what has been experienced or said. I am using the word story to encourage others to recognise that they too have a story to tell about themselves, and not to be fearful of doing so.

In my work with clients, I find that they are not always able to tell me initially, but what they are unable to say can have the most profound effect upon them. My skills lie in my ability to create a safe and caring environment. A place where each person's uniqueness can be respected and honoured, so that they can say what to them until then has been unspeakable. I see clients who are successful in their own right but, when it comes to telling their own deeply personal stories, they are unable to begin, to even shape the words with their mouth, let alone to tell the story that is most intimate to them.

Having said this, the unspeakable does in fact communicate itself in other ways than through the voice. It communicates itself through controlled or controlling behaviour, or through uncontrolled or obsessive behaviour, through phobias or various addictions, or other physical manifestations like depression, stress, anxiety or illness.

Often it is only when these forms of communication no longer accommodate the person's emotional needs, or they feel they are different and therefore possibly losing their sanity, that they seek out a counsellor or psychotherapist in order to work with their story. I am not suggesting here that these behaviours do represent insanity, but what I am saying is that, sadly, although we live in a world that recognises difference through ethnicity, age, gender, sexuality, religion and class, we still live in a conformist society as far as people's mindsets are concerned.

It is at this point that the VOICE becomes the point of entry into this often feared and unrecognised internal landscape from which each person's individual story comes. Using the power of speech can eventually enable them to link body, mind and spirit so that the wounds they have been unable to speak of before can be healed. The courage to face ourselves in our own silence. The highly respected Jungian psychotherapist Marion Woodman says 'silence taught me to hear my soul'. It is with this in mind that I encourage anyone to find their voice, to free themselves to be the unique person that they truly are.

The power of the voice and the use of language is fundamental to our well-being, our creativity and our ability to have power over our experiences, our values and our ideas. Our voice gives us the power to be heard and to be respected.'

One example of this comes from Helen, a highly successful businesswoman, trainer and author. She was interviewed for a documentary series I did on domestic abuse.

'Some days, when I'm feeling confident and good about myself, I can find my own voice and articulate what I want to have heard with no trouble. And there are other days (we all have the odd dark day) when the past catches up with me and for one reason or another I am not managing my inner dialogue very well; on those days I don't find it easy to express myself. Mind you, it is important for me to recognise that the more habituated I get to using my own voice, the more confident I become and the easier it is to express myself, even on the dark days. It is all about developing habits that support me in life and ditching the ones that don't.

When I look back over my life and ask myself when I found my own voice, I find it hard to pinpoint an exact moment of realisation. I can name particular events when I know I stood up for myself and even though I was quaking in my boots on occasion, I still knew that I had said my piece and I had been heard. I came away from those moments feeling triumphant and proud of myself. There have been other times when what has happened can only be described as someone other than me speaking for me. It was as though the voice came from nowhere, from behind me somehow. I realise now that when I speak straight from my heart, not my mind, the truth will out, so to speak, whether I meant to say it or not!

One of those occasions was when Joanna asked me to participate in a series of programmes on domestic violence and I heard myself say "yes" and then asked myself who had uttered that word "yes". (I'm very glad I did participate, by the way, because what she offered me was an opportunity to find my voice and speak my truth publicly.)

I was brought up in a country where boys are rated and girls are not. Our nanny doted on my little brother, who could do no wrong, whereas she used to punish me, to the point of torturing me, at the drop of a hat. I grew up with the firmly entrenched belief that boys are better than girls and that if you want to get on in life it would be infinitely easier if you were a boy. (Incidentally that belief ruled my life until very recently.) My first recollections of not being heard are of early childhood, when I complained to my parents about the nanny, was told I was talking nonsense, and was summarily despatched to my room. This led to my developing tantrums as a means of getting attention. I can still feel the frustration of not being listened to in my body now. So, the pattern was established very early on: boys are better than girls and people don't listen to girls.

We all know about the concept of mind games, but perhaps we don't give our own minds enough credit for their ability to interfere with what is really important, namely what our hearts want. The mind is a very, very powerful thing and will (in my experience) take every opportunity it can to divert me from where I really want to go or what I really want to say. Fear lives in the past. We feel fear as a result of our past experience; it is very little to do with what is yet to come. The fear of what we have known in the past gets projected onto the future; that then allows us to be afraid of the future. But the future is unknown, there's no fear there – we haven't been there yet! Once I recognised that, I was able to move on and find the courage to express myself.

I was the victim ('was' being the operative word) of domestic abuse and violence in more than one set of circumstances. Until a few years ago, the belief that boys are better than girls still ruled. What this meant in effect was that I allowed myself to be abused because it fitted the old childhood pattern. Then two things happened: one was the realisation that I needed to take responsibility for the fact that I was allowing the abuse to be perpetuated; and the other was the discovery that I didn't deserve it. The two are inextricably linked.

Once I started taking responsibility I was able to take back my power rather than giving it away. I was able to source my own life – to be the author of the circumstances of my choice, rather than being at the mercy of someone else's. The discovery strengthened my resolve and I began to value myself more as a result. By valuing myself more, my self-esteem grew, and that is where I found the courage to break the old patterns and begin to create new ones. I became acutely aware that if you see yourself as a victim, you will always attract an oppressor. By being a victim, you allow someone to keep doing what they have always done, so they keep doing it! Why wouldn't they? It was time to give up being a victim and to take charge of my life.

Life is different now. I value who I am and my contribution to the people I love and the people I work with. If I hadn't had the courage to break out I wouldn't be able to contribute to them in the way that I know I do, because half of me (at least) wasn't on the playing field. My relationships with my daughters have been transformed, my grandsons are learning to respect women and I am much better at my job. Result! And, believe me, that is worth every ounce of the fear and discomfort that I experienced along the way.

I feel that is important to point out that no two stories or sets of circumstances are the same. This is my story, you will have your own, and I acknowledge and honour yours. What I do know is that one of the frequent cases of abuse, whether you are the abuser or the abused, is low self-esteem. Valuing yourself, growing your self-worth, telling yourself that you deserve better, is the way toward finding your own voice. If you keep telling yourself you are crap that is what you will be. If you keep telling yourself that you are worthy of a better life, the chances are that that is what you will create. It is a journey well worth embarking on and, when you do, the dark days become fewer and fewer as your voice gets louder and louder.'

RECOVERY THROUGH FINDING YOUR VOICE

One in ten of the population is said to be suffering from a life-threatening addiction of one form or another. It seems modern society is uncovering an ever-growing list of substances or behaviours that certain people have a propensity to be addicted to and that illness can lead to their downfall.

Addiction is viewed by those in the know as an illness of the mind, body and spirit. A disease of the emotions, or rather dis-ease with oneself, where the addict is constantly seeking to escape from themselves or the realities of their life through mood-altering substances.

There are lots of so-called cures out there, but millions of addicts throughout the world have been helped by a programme that is based on talking about one's behaviour and feelings to other addicts who can identify with them, which in turn helps the addict to stay sober or clean. In this context, using one's voice to speak out is literally life-saving.

Rupert, who's 33, has been clean of drugs for eight years. He puts his recovery down to talking about his addiction and being honest.

'When I look at my last days of drug using, to the outside world it was abundantly clear that I had a problem and yet I was still trying to hide the truth from them.

Eventually, for whatever reason, I admitted I had a problem not just to myself but to somebody else. That act of actually saying to someone else 'I've got a problem' was the beginning. The weight that came off my shoulders at that time was literally incredible.

I went to drug rehab, where we were encouraged to speak about all the things that we'd never told anyone. All the awful secrets, the guilt and shame we had carried for years. That could be, for example, what I'd actually done with all the money my parents had given me. The extent to which drugs ruled my life and how long they'd ruled my life for. When I spoke about the harm and damage I had caused my family and friends and the reality about how I felt about myself for behaving like that, it helped me to realise that everything I experienced and felt about myself – others felt like that too.

Speaking out meant facing myself and others. It set a precedent for a new way to live my life. In that honesty I got the help and support I needed to get well. Since then it's not pills or mood-altering substances I turn to, but dealing with issues that need to be dealt with.

In order to find your voice, you have to realise you've lost it in the first place and only then can you set about trying to work out how to use it. For 21 years I suffered in silence, never willing to speak my truth and, perhaps more importantly, never admitting the truth to myself.

The effect of keeping quiet ultimately brought me to my knees and I'm in no doubt that, if today I behaved in the same way, I'd fall down again.

The things I have problems with aren't earth-shattering, in fact they're part and parcel of everyday life. It's just that I'm a proud person and don't like to admit that everything in the house isn't rosy all of the time. But the reality for most people is that not every day is a good one and sometimes those bad days turn into weeks. The important thing is to make sure those weeks don't turn into years or, for me, more importantly, to ensure I don't turn to something chemical for help.

If I never told anyone the causes of my low points the results would be messy. It's just like a company keeping secrets from its shareholders. Generally the firm would only do that if the information it wanted to protect was negative. The fact is the truth usually comes out in the end and, when it does, it's bound to be a lot more painful than if it had been released earlier.

In my life the shareholders are the people around me. My family, my girlfriend, my friends, my employer. All of them have an interest in my well-being, as I do in theirs. All those relationships need work to maintain and that doesn't mean burying my head in the sand and blindly hoping that things will improve. It means confronting the problems that arise in order to ensure they don't get worse.

And that's what using my voice means to me. I may not like confrontation but equally it's the confrontation that will keep me sane. Sometimes the issues I need to face are so trivial they hardly seem worth bothering about. But it's better to tackle them than face the consequences of inaction.

For some reason that I don't know the answer to, I spent two thirds of my life keeping quiet. I wasn't silent, just silent on certain subjects, mainly how I felt about the world around me. Consequently I was on a fast track to hell, fuelled by a cocktail of drink and drugs. Eventually and fortunately I was rescued and was taught that it was OK to speak out. My life has only ever got better since then.'

CHILDREN'S VOICES

We should be concerned about how we communicate in all areas of our life. Most parents will no doubt agree that it is sometimes very difficult to get our message across to our children. They either don't hear or don't want to hear us; or perhaps it's sometimes down to the fact we don't hear them. Truth, honesty and clarity are good foundation stones for any communication with one's family. If things aren't said clearly, the wrong messages can be picked up.

Emotional intelligence is being hailed as a powerful communication tool in any context. In other words, being aware of our own emotional sensitivities and those of others, and being able to manage our feelings rather than letting our feelings manage us.

Sarah Walters is a professional herbalist who specialises in working with children.

'I wanted to be a vet when I was younger and I ended up a herbal practitioner, which has become my passion as well as my job. I always believed that health should be encompassed holistically. This basically means that you take into account the mind, body and the spirit of people, knowing that these are all connected and affect each other. My other lovely job is looking after children and that's probably why I chose to specialise in children's healthcare.

Children are blessed with weird and wonderful ideas, and it is my belief that within safe boundaries these should always be expressed, tried and tested! In my work as a herbalist one of the key tools which I can use is communication. If a parent brings their child to see me I always spend the first half of the session talking to the child, assuming they are old enough to express themselves, and with small babies I spend time talking and playing with them. This unconsciously forms a bond and hopefully a feeling of trust; only then can healing really take place.

The voice is a wonderful tool, it can express empathy, offer sympathy, show delight, encourage optimism, and helps to set up a trusting relationship between you and the child. The key is to try and connect on some level by changing the tone of voice or the words that you speak. Children respond well to humour, but they also appreciate honesty. They understand an enormous amount of conversation, sometimes just from a tone of voice rather than spoken words. Children have many ways to attract our attention and be heard, and yet some find this more difficult than others. There is no set way to communicate, the challenge is to reach an understanding of each other on a one-to-one basis.

In herbal treatment the aim is not just to take away the symptoms of illness, but to rebalance the body according to unique individual needs and to encourage optimum health in mind, body and spirit.

For children this is especially important to allow them to develop, grow, have confidence and be comfortable with who they are. A child's illness can often have profound effects on their relationship with parents and siblings. So it can provide the opportunity for close bonding as well as change and development in a really positive way.

So instead of seeing an illness as a negative setback, I see it as a sign that some change needs to be implemented, either mentally, emotionally or physically – or all three! And more often than not this means communicating and understanding.

How wonderful the love, strength, confidence and courage the spoken word can give.'

BIBLIOGRAPHY

Buzan, Tony, *How to Mind Map: the Ultimate Thinking Tool that will Change your Life*, HarperCollins, 2002

Colclough, Beechy and Josephine, *A Challenge to Change*, Thorsons, 1999

Cole, Kris, *The Complete Idiot's Guide to Clear Communication*, Alpha Books, 2002

Dewhurst-Maddock, Olivea, *Healing with Sound*, Gaia Books, 1997

Dickson, Anne, *A Woman in Your Own Right*, Quartet Books, 1982

Hay, Louise, *You Can Heal Your Life* (paperback edition), Full Circle Publishing, 2003

Hobday, Peter, *Managing the Message*, London House, 2000

Minns, Sue, *Be Your Own Soul Doctor*, Cico Books, 2002

Morris, Desmond, *Peoplewatching, The Desmond Morris Guide to Body Language*, Vintage, 2002

Nicholls, Anne, *Mastering Public Speaking*, How to Books, 1999

Pease, Allan, *Body Language: How to Read Others' Attitudes by their Gestures*, Orion, 2003

Stuart, Christina, *Speak For Yourself*, Piatkus Books, 2001

Turner, Diane, and Greco, Thelma, *The Personality Compass*, Thorsons, 2001

CONTACTS

Gary Owston, ACTION – Voice in Action
owston@madasafish.com
Tel: 0117 962 6277 / 0208 7642763

Lyn Macnab, Integrative Counsellor and Psychotherapist
lynnab@supanet.com
Tel: 01749 831 328

Steve Brodie, Home Affairs Correspondent, BBC Bristol
Steve.brodie@bbc.co.uk

Steve Egginton, Head of News, ITV West
Steve.egginton@itv.com

Jane Alexander, Journalist and author
www.janealexander.org
jane@janealexander.org